SACRED
Knowing

CHÉRIE LINDBERG, PHD

Table of Contents

Dedication

To Kim Goffin,

Your passing opened doors in my heart and in my life that I never saw coming.

What a strange and sacred gift grief can be.

Your spirit continues to whisper truths that guide me home to myself.

Thank you for walking beside me then, and somehow…still now.

To my husband, Paul,

Your love has been my foundation.

For all thirty-six years of our marriage, you've been there—quietly, faithfully—cheering me on at the base of every mountain I've ever decided to climb.

This book wouldn't exist without you and your unwavering belief in me.

To my sons,

Yes, I know you think your mom is kind of weird.

But I also know you love me, and I feel that, deeply.

Becoming your mother cracked me open. You taught me to face myself, my triggers, and to stretch into the kind of presence I wanted you to grow up with. I'm better because of you. Still a work in process as well. Thank you for your patience.

CHÉRIE LINDBERG, PHD

To my colleagues,

Thank you for holding space when I was scared and uncertain.

For bearing witness as I prepared to share work that demands visibility, vulnerability, and deep trust.

You gave me courage.

To David Grand,

Your mentorship has shaped me more than you know.

To Lisa Williams,

Thank you for seeing the healing potential in this method and helping bring it into the light. Your encouragement reminded me that spiritual work is meant to be shared.

To my readers,

Even if I'm not your cup of tea, I still appreciate your presence here.

Even criticism is a form of engagement, and that takes effort.

I don't need you to agree with everything in these pages. But I do hope, if even only for a moment, you feel something real.

To my mother, father, sister, and brother,

You gave me the first space to grow, to stumble, to rise.

I learned more than I could have named at the time, and for that, I am deeply grateful. I continue with the lessons in our family and in our lineage.

To my Peruvian brothers and the many teachers who have helped shape my spiritual path,

Your guidance lives in these words.

To the Earth beneath my feet, to the wisdom of the animals, and to the solace of the natural world,

Thank you for holding me during my hardest seasons. You reminded me that healing never happens in isolation. May you who read this book be touched by something deeper than words.

May you receive exactly what your soul is ready for.

May we all continue to grow toward the next evolution of our being, together, and in love. With infinite gratitude,

—Cherie Lindberg, PhD

Words from Colleagues

Cherie's timely, thoughtful, inspiring book comes at an important time in the evolution of brainspotting as it contributes and adds to the Neuroexperiental Model (NEM) of Brainspotting. One of the core tenets of the NEM is that culture comes before (Western) science. This can naturally be extended to the statement that spirituality comes before science.

In my own development as a therapeutic healer, I've experienced many therapists and model developers look askance at the role of spirituality in the process of healing trauma. It is notable that cultures and communities around the globe, that have existed for hundreds and thousands of years, have spiritual practices and healing beliefs, even with no communication with each other. Perhaps this came about with their tapping into collective ancestors holding shared intuitive wisdom. This sense of knowing is intertwined with the sense of (human) being. brainspotting's NEM is open to, values and seeks out these global, indigenous beliefs and practices.

I have been honored to be an integral part of Cherie's brainspotting, sacred, spiritual, evolutionary and meaning-seeking journey sourcing back to her sojourn with me that she aptly describes in her book. Her journey derives from and contributes to my journey and as such the larger expansion of the NEM. Her translucent chronicling of her journeys is both fascinating, uplifting and inspiring.

Most important of all, is how it provides a sacred roadmap that can encourage and role model for the spiritual journey of the reader in and out of the global brainspotting evolution. It will be both rewarding and uplifting to see where this individual and collective expansive journey takes you.

– David Grand, PhD
August 2025

I'm healed… until I'm triggered.

That line has become my mantra, a reminder that healing isn't a finish line, it's a lifelong practice. No matter how much work I've done, there will always be moments that catch me off guard, stir up old wounds, and invite me to go deeper. Being triggered doesn't mean I've failed; it means I'm human. It means I'm still growing.

Over the past three decades, I've worked in the spiritual industry as a psychic medium, speaking to more than seven million people and training over 35,000 students worldwide to access their intuition. I've sat in ceremonies that cracked me open, walked with others through their darkest nights, and experienced profound healing of my own. And still, all it takes is one trigger to remind me: the work never ends.

When I met Cherie, I felt an immediate resonance. We connected a few years ago through a course I was teaching, and what first bound us together was our shared fascination with neuroscience. She spoke about her work with brainspotting, and while it sounded simple, even odd at first, something in me trusted her enough to say yes to a session. That trust changed everything.

What I thought would be a surface-level issue, frustration over my son not returning my calls, opened into something I had buried for 45 years: a childhood memory that had silently shaped my financial narrative and the way I made decisions as an adult. I had worked with sacred plant medicine over the years, which had touched deep places within myself, and received visions and downloads that changed me. But this memory had stayed locked away, untouched even in those powerful ceremonies.

In my session with Cherie, brainspotting created a safe and compassionate space that allowed that memory to surface finally. The emotions came with it, and for the first time, I didn't just recall the experience; I healed it. That moment reminded me that our bodies and souls know how to heal if only we give them permission.

That session cracked me open, and it was only the beginning. I went on to train in brainspotting myself and integrate it into my work, but what stayed with me most was how Cherie held space: grounded, clear, and compassionate. She made the process feel not only safe but sacred. And that is who she is, not just a practitioner of a technique, but a guide who bridges science and spirituality in a way that is rare and deeply needed.

Because here's the bigger truth: this book is not just about brainspotting. It is about spiritual practices that can heal, reconnect us to our intuition, and remind us who we are beneath the layers of fear, trauma, and conditioning. Cherie invites us to embrace these practices as daily medicine, whether they come through brainspotting, meditation, ceremony, movement, or prayer.

I've seen firsthand how such practices open people. In my own work, I've witnessed clients uncover ancestral patterns that had weighed down generations, connect with past life memories that explained lifelong fears, and discover for the first time the sacred voice of their own intuition. Cherie has also witnessed this. Her work serves as a reminder that healing is not just about releasing trauma; it is about reclaiming wholeness.

Cherie embodies this balance of the mystical and the practical. She is both a scientist and a seeker, grounded in research yet unafraid to speak of the spirit. She understands that intuition is not reserved for a gifted few; it is a birthright, available to all of us if we are willing to slow down, listen, and practice. She doesn't teach from theory but from her own lived experience, her own moments of being cracked open, her own courage to face what many would rather avoid. That is what makes her voice so trustworthy.

And she tells the truth: healing isn't always neat or pretty. It is messy, it is raw, and sometimes it will bring you to your knees. It will ask you to face memories you'd rather keep buried and emotions you'd rather not feel. It will show you that you're not as healed as you thought you were. And that's okay. Because healing isn't about perfection. It is about honesty. It is about courage. It is about showing up for yourself again and again, even when it's hard.

That is why this book matters. It isn't a quick fix or a surface-level self-help guide. It is an initiation. A roadmap. A sacred container for your own remembering. Cherie offers you a way back home, to your intuition, to your spirit, to the wisdom and wholeness that have always lived inside you.

If you're holding this book right now, maybe you're curious. Maybe you're skeptical. Maybe you've tried everything else and you're wondering if this could finally be the thing that helps. Wherever you are, welcome.

Here's what I can promise: if you allow yourself to step into this journey with an open heart and mind, something will shift. Maybe it will be subtle. Maybe it will be seismic. But it will be real.

Because the work Cherie shares has a way of bypassing our defenses and going straight to the core. It doesn't demand, it invites. It doesn't force, it reveals.

So yes, I'm healed… until I'm triggered.

And thanks to practices like the ones Cherie shares, when those triggers arise, I now have tools that help me navigate them with compassion, courage, and grace.

Cherie is the guide I trust on this path. And by the time you finish this book, I believe you will too.

Take a breath. Lean in. And get ready to meet parts of yourself you may not have seen in years, maybe ever. They've been waiting for you.

May this book remind you of the wisdom that has always lived within you. May it be a doorway back to your intuition, your spirit, and your wholeness.

- Lisa Williams, *Author, teacher and spiritual leader*
masterinstructor@lisawilliams.com
LISAWILLIAMS.COM
August 2025

My Integrated Mind and Spiritual Journey

I started, like most mental health professionals, by working on my traumas and post-traumatic stress disorder (PTSD). In that, I found myself revealing, then removing my biases. My journey has had many influences, from my time as a therapist and coaching others, which has led me from being a simple therapist to a transformational coach.

In my healing journey, brainspotting played a key role in helping me overcome personal challenges, and in turn, inspired me to pursue a professional career in brainspotting. Now, it's not only my profession, but a spiritual tool to guide my daily life.

Perhaps it's ironic, but I believe my traumas and my childhood experience compelled me to help others. This is not uncommon among health service providers.

Growing up, I was always a spiritual kid, frequently labeled "the weirdo" in school. With few good friends growing up, the pressures of being rejected added to my already existing traumas, leading me to shut people out. After nearly ten years of losing close friends and even family members to this, I found the courage to build a community again. It felt like a risk, putting myself into a vulnerable position once more.

We live in a blaming and shaming society, pushing us to repress ourselves, not speak our minds, and constantly fear being judged. For some of us, this removes the ability to stay connected when there's conflict, so we resort to our coping and defense mechanisms, assigning blame to others without evaluating why the *thing we're blaming* is triggering us.

Everyone wants to be themselves freely, without fear of being judged or shamed; yet, most of us prefer to assign blame to others rather than work on our own issues. Interpersonal relationships and having a strong sense of community require compassion and acceptance. Most of us are unaware of blaming the programming we grew up with. It doesn't even occur to us to work on it, or we are afraid of what our community might think of us working on these skills. I know that I can speak up about my feelings and thoughts because my community members are welcoming and tolerant. At least these days they are.

When I was young, I didn't feel like I had a safe space to talk about my needs. I desperately wanted a large family, but when I told my family my desires and traumas, it backfired on me. I lost my family. It was rough, especially for a young kid. Later on, as I started to learn about myself and continued to follow my spiritual beliefs, I kept quiet about everything. I knew I couldn't trust my family members again with my truth. I feared a reprisal; they were going to judge me again. It wasn't until I got my degrees that knowledge gave me the confidence to be free, feeling safe to come out and show my true self again.

My journey is not unique. A lot of people hide who they really are out of fear, especially young people. When we're young, we discover ourselves—experimenting with new things, consuming different content, trying different identities on. Initially, some of these things will make us feel seen or recognized. However, when we bring these new ideas and perspectives into our communities, sometimes they're disregarded or labeled as negative, making us inhibit ourselves and hide our true selves. This becomes an issue as we try to figure out how we belong and fit into our confusing world—into our communities and societies. To break the cycle of blame and create a safe space in our communities, someone needs to show compassion. I hope that after reading this book, that someone is *you*.

A Fearless Child

I'm writing this book because I want to be fearless, but being fearless is scary! Contradictory, I know. Becoming fearless begins with vulnerability, and that doesn't come easily. We need each other to become fearless; we are social creatures at the end of the day. Our spirits are connected as a collective to help each other out—to bring light where there is darkness. We rely on one another to succeed—to exist. As a child, I was absolutely annihilated, but through healing and knowledge, I have overcome trauma and am now confident in my personal power. This is something I often see in women, as we grow away from repressive systems and relationships, although men often undergo similar experiences recovering from these same repressive systems.

My First Exploration of Other Dimensions

After becoming a professional, I took a huge risk and went to Ecuador for my first brainspotting intensive with David Grand. Essentially a master class to develop advanced skills as a clinical brainspotting therapist and trainer, these intensive sessions often take place in international locations, with registration limited to just ten participants. A small, intimate group where we take turns being both the therapist and the client.

So, I joined the intensive group in Ecuador, but still, I was on my own. In a space where I had one colleague with me, the rest of the attendees did not know me. This was scary, but I trusted David. During my healing practice, spiritual beings started to show up. This was all new to me; I was spiritual, yes, but I hadn't connected to spirits like this before. But when three flowy, 13-plus-foot-tall spiritual beings show themselves to you, you start to question your sanity. The spirits were receptive and open to sharing information with me.

The spiritual being told me I had a gift that I could transmute negative energy in large groups. That I was directly connected to the divine and that I could use this energy to help people heal. Every spectator at the time was in awe, and at the end of the session, the translator and a woman came up to me and said, "You know you were channeling *A Course in Miracles*, right?"

She left me in shock. Yes, I knew *of* the book, but I had never read it. I still haven't to this day. Back then, I was still a big skeptic, so despite my surprise, I poo-pooed the idea of spiritual beings appearing and me reciting a book I had never read. I blamed the whole event on myself, accusing myself of hallucinating things. But after that, the spirits continued to show themselves to me. For the longest time, I ignored them and the feelings they produced in me. I was afraid and kept repeating to myself that I was making it all up. It couldn't be real…but it was, and continues to be so.

My Spiritual Awakening

Three years ago, during my lunch break, while I was doing a brainspotting training, I received a call from my best friend Kim's husband saying, "I don't know if she is dead or alive."

But I knew. I knew she had passed away because her spirit had appeared on my right side. I could see her, and I knew spiritual appearances only come from the deceased. I was perplexed. I didn't know what to do, say, or act. I most definitely couldn't tell him I was seeing his dead wife right next to me. I didn't even know how I was going to make it through the rest of the training. All I could do at that moment was to try to listen to him. I kept saying I was sorry and reassured him that he was doing everything he *could* do. After we got off the phone, still frozen by my friend's appearance and news of her death, I went to my fellow trainer, Cynthia, for advice, and she suggested that we brainspot Kim's spirit. I agreed.

We got right into it. I was very nervous, but I needed answers. We ended up brainspotting and talking to Kim's spirit for an hour. She told me she left Earth the way she wanted; she didn't want her family to see her slowly deteriorate or for them to see her suffer. She told me she was ready to leave the living world. She told me she loved me, and that she would take care of my loved ones transitioning into the spiritual world when their time came if I'd take care of hers on Earth. My parents and elderly loved ones would be protected thanks to Kim.

During the last moments of our conversation, she told me, "You need to become a death doula and start doing more spiritual work."

At the time, I didn't know what being a *death doula* meant, so I looked it up and immediately thought, "Oh no, I don't want to do that." But literally, two weeks after her passing, I received an email for a collaboration invite from a death doula. She wanted to work with me; she had looked for me. It was chilling, and I remember thinking, "Kim, knock it off. I'm not doing this!" But Kim knew better. She already knew where my professional strengths would be needed the most.

While brainspotting with Kim, I could feel her, I could even smell her, weird as that is. Kim and I embraced each other in a hug, and I was able to say my proper goodbye. I was supposed to go the following week to visit her, but our meeting was paid in advance. I was able to finish the training with my colleague and was grateful for this experience.

The next day, on an inspiring Sunday morning, I woke up determined. I finished the third day of the training and decided I was finished with trauma work. From now on, I was going to do coaching, where I could fully explore the spiritual side of myself and my clients. On Monday morning, I called all my clients. I told them that in three months, I would be shutting the counseling doors and opening a coaching practice instead. I rebranded my business and image, and since then, I've been working full-time for a diverse clientele offering high-performance coaching, consulting, and teaching brainspotting. The experience with Kim changed my life forever. I am focused more on posttraumatic growth, spiritually, and flourishing work now.

Before Kim's funeral, I brainspotted with her again. Her family wanted me to give a speech at her funeral, not knowing that I could ask her directly what she wanted me to say, I asked her for help. I found a beautiful poem I thought sensible for the funeral, and Kim helped me tweak it. We ended up writing about her father and brother and their estranged relationship. Kim's funeral was the first time they had been together in years, and through the poem, we spoke about that.

I spoke before the crowd:

> John 14:1-3
> Jesus Comforts His Disciples
> "Do not let your hearts be troubled. You believe in God; believe also in me. My Father's house has many rooms; if that were not so, would I have told you that I am going there to prepare a place for you? And if I go and prepare a place for you, I will come back and take you to be with me that you also may be where I am."
> At the rising of the sun and as it is going down,
> We will remember you, Kim.
> At the blowing of the wind and in the chill of Winter,
> We will remember you, Kim.
> At the opening of buds and in the rebirth of Spring,
> We will remember you, Kim.
> At the blueness of the skies and in the warmth of Summer,
> We will remember you, Kim.
> At the rustling of leaves and the beauty of Autumn,
> We will remember you, Kim.
> At the beginning of the year and when it ends,
> We will remember you, Kim.
> As long as we live, you too will live within us, Kim, as you.
> You are now a part of everyone you have ever touched.
> This is the time to wake up and reflect on your life. Kim would want us to put our defenses down and tell our friends and family we love them.
> Let there be comfort in knowing she was at peace with God as she faced her eternal rest. Let there be peace inside your heart,

as she loved and cared for everyone in this room and everyone she knew that touched her life.

Let her sweet heart and life be a message to open your heart. She would want this for all of us. Let us spend time together this afternoon celebrating her life.

Love and light to you, sweet angel, until we meet again, my dear friend.

My Interdisciplinary Approach to Spirits

Kim led me to experiences I had never considered before, either because I wasn't comfortable with them, attracted to them, or even aware of them! She's the reason why I opened more and more to the spiritual world and finally became a believer. Despite my initial apprehension about working in the spiritual world, my experiences and brainspotting with Kim inspired me to accept working with the doula and those transitioning.

I had been attending group sessions with an incredible medium for some time. He, the medium, was sure I was very gifted, and I couldn't believe I was reading people so accurately. I thought that they were all pretending my talent and efforts were successful because the skeptic in me could not accept what was happening. Seeing, hearing, talking, feeling, and smelling spirits? Yeah, right. That couldn't *actually* be happening. For me, it was impossible, and I didn't understand where all of the spirit talking was going, so I stopped attending the meetings.

I wasn't sure if including this story now would have any impact on this book, but in all honesty, I keep crossing paths with individuals who are attracted to my work at my training sessions who have these gifts too. In my experience, speaking about my spiritual experiences allows many others the confidence to share their experiences as well. Eventually, this helped me normalize my spiritual endeavors, and ultimately, compelled me to write this book from a spiritual perspective rather than a strictly scientific one.

As soon as I decided to write a book about my healing journey and my practice, my spiritual committee immediately showed up to me; they asked me not to forget them in this moment. I quickly reassured them that they are part of my journey, and therefore, part of this book.

Recently, I met a woman from Sweden. We've been talking for quite some time through LinkedIn, and finally, agreed to meet over Zoom, and performed a quantum healing out of this freaking universe. Through our conversations, it's like speaking a language that five years ago we wouldn't have had the vocabulary to speak, related to healing and finding information in other dimensions to help us restore our trinity balance, mind, body, and spirit.

To be accepted by our society, it would seem the Neuroexperiential Model of Brainspotting has to be academically and scientifically oriented, as most are still skeptics about the spiritual realm. However, the Neuroexperiential Model is open to indigenous knowledge and spirituality. To me, the spiritual realm feels like a portal to our souls, a way to creatively highlight our true essence beyond cultural norms and society's accepted programming. The full spectrum of my journey, I guess, started out in conventional logical land, working on my PTSD through therapy, and using brainspotting as a method to overcome my traumas. But now, it's the spiritual tools that guide my daily life. I see a brain spot as a portal to getting access to the spiritual realm, as well as to our ancestors' wisdom.

CHAPTER 2

Attachment and Attunement

The Past is in the Present

Many people I encounter in sessions ask themselves: Why am I here? Why am I reacting this way? Why do I feel this way? But in answering those questions, they have to confront the part their past has to play in those feelings; they say, "I don't want to go back there; that's over with." But in actuality, that's not the case.

I often say the brain and body are historical organs because the past is not truly in the past. It carries through to the present via both mind and body. Trauma is imprinted in our nervous systems, and if not healed, gets triggered in the present. These systems hold your past experiences in your body, and these manifest in your behavior when provoked and remembered. You must understand where your past experiences come from to identify the root. To achieve this, you need to delve deeper into the brain and body, reprocessing and releasing old experiences and narratives. Only then can your body learn to let go and shift to make intentional choices to do things differently. Those intentional choices and decisions are establishing new narratives, new boundaries, and new patterns. The ability to self-reflect and redirect is a learned skill of discernment. This is you waking up to the present, to the person you are evolving into.

As clients and practitioners, it is key to the healing journey to accept the past and how it affects the present. As practitioners, we have to make sure that no matter what modality we are using, we're not bringing our personal past into our professional processes. Even though we all do it anyway, we try to clear out as much bias as possible so that if I'm leading with my higher self, the client is able to grow deeper and faster into theirs. But if I'm still blocked, which, in brainspotting, we call limbic countertransference, I may get in the way of the client's process because of my own past. This may impact my ability to hold space and attune to my client's system.

So, although it may not be attainable to completely absolve yourself of your personal journey when helping your clients, it is key to maintain the boundaries of leading with your highest self in respect of your practice and their progress.

If you don't learn practices to release and regulate yourself daily, secondary trauma accumulates in your own systems in your neurobiology. This isn't about achieving perfection but about making progress while preventing burnout. Once burnout sets in, you'll unconsciously project your biases and traumas onto the client, or whoever you interact with. This accumulation is known as vicarious trauma and secondary exposure. These occur when we absorb the trauma material we hear, and our physiology responds by recreating those triggered feelings.

By recognizing and managing how these experiences manifest in our thoughts and behaviors, we can remain impartial and receptive, creating a supportive space for the client. Otherwise, a triggered therapist is more likely to intervene during a brainspotting process prematurely. A healer reacting from their own fear may interrupt the process, preventing the client from reaching the depth of exploration they need to fully heal.

Attachment and Attunement

Attunement can be understood as sitting with another person and engaging with them, harmonizing, resonating, adapting, and syncing up to their energy. Whether through eye contact, listening, or just being present, attunement is engaging relationally and neurobiologically with another person. This ability is a cornerstone of brainspotting. People benefit when they feel that a practitioner attunes to them and that they're present. In this process, the limbic systems sync up, co-regulate, and merge, allowing for a mutual understanding in the present moment that supports the client wherever they need to go.

Attachment is interlinked with the attunement process. Attachment styles are the basic patterns of how you show up in your relationships based on childhood relationships with caregivers. The styles can fit into two umbrella categories: secure and insecure.

Secure attachment translates as a healthy social capability in fostering and maintaining relationships. Insecure attachment styles are ways of adapting to survive in relationships. The insecure attachment styles include anxious, avoidant, and disorganized. In determining styles, the attachment process begins when we come out of the womb; we have caregivers who attune to and care for us. The attachments from a person's first connections mold our autonomic and central nervous systems, shaping how our brain begins to organize core experiences and core beliefs about the world. It's like we put on a pair of glasses synced with a view of the world as it has been developed for us by the caregivers.

Attachment styles are connected to emotional regulation, which stems from synchronized healthy responses between child and caregiver. If we have a caregiver who is very loving and looks at us in love, we then develop a secure attachment to them and the world. In turn, we organize the world around us as safe, and as a part of the world, "I am lovable and cared for".

Opposingly, people who have experienced childhood trauma are more susceptible to the detriments of insecure attachment styles. If a caregiver is inconsistent, possibly in the case of a depressed parent, the child will take on an anxious attachment and form a belief that the world will behave as their caregivers have, inconsistently and with uncertainty.

Avoidant attachment stems from experiencing early relationships that had angrily critical and dismissive tendencies. People with this style of attachment often withdraw from intimacy and deny their own feelings to appease others. The pattern of self-deflection and appeasing can invoke the mentality of "sometimes the world is safe, sometimes I'm lovable, sometimes I will be taken care of."

Disorganized attachment is the third sector of insecure attachment styles, deriving from the parent having been a source of terror for the child. At the core, the person internalizes the belief that says, "I am worthless, I am not lovable, and the world is not safe." This is more trauma-based because some kind of abuse occurred. As a result, our system develops dissociative and dysregulatory tendencies in an attempt to adapt.

These adaptations become our defense mechanisms, shaping how we navigate life. If we don't recognize them, we risk carrying the same attachment and attunement patterns we developed at five years old into adulthood. This is a key reason why many relationships struggle. Partners often lack emotional regulation due to unresolved attachment issues. In essence, they replay their past trauma with each other, unconsciously reenacting old patterns.

Like magnets, we attract people who reinforce our core beliefs and reflect behaviors we expect from the world. Breaking this cycle requires intentional change, which can feel uncomfortable because the familiar, even when unhealthy, feels safe.

Here is where brainspotting can play a role. Through attunement, the practitioner helps facilitate attachment repair, allowing you to reparent yourself from within. You begin to recognize that these deeply held beliefs were simply adaptations to past experiences, patterns that once served you but no longer do.

In time, this process creates an internal shift, integrating the brain for greater balance rather than operating from a trauma-driven state. As a result, new possibilities open up, creatively, spiritually, and emotionally, allowing you to move forward and evolve into your true, authentic self.

Brainspotting is a journey with no set ending, fluctuating, and reliant on the inner being of the participant. So, attachment styles are reflective of the basic pattern of how you show up in a relationship based on what it was like in your relationships that influenced you as a child with your caregivers.

We keep reenacting the past because our soul is trying to heal, just not in an effective way. We are doing this as a collective society as well. If we can't wake up and realize these patterns, as a society, we will keep seeing the world as the problem. Instead of realizing, "Wait a minute, these are old wounds I'm getting access to; this is growth trying to happen!"

Even though it doesn't feel very good at times, the process of waking up can change our lives, culture, and society. Our souls are always trying to evolve. Becoming conscious and working with our history helps us heal and show up as our best selves.

Brainspotting

Brainspotting is a parts approach. Brainspotting helped me reconnect with the little girl inside me who believed she could do anything, rejuvenating the energy within me that had been suppressed. So invested in this transformational process, within the first two years of practicing it personally and with clients, my colleagues and I, along with a group of practitioners, founded the Midwest Brainspotting Institute. I was first trained in Eye Movement Desensitization and Reprocessing (EMDR), and it significantly reduced my PTSD symptoms. While the EMDR reduced my symptoms, brainspotting made my soul come alive! From there, I opened my private practice and trained 11 people in brainspotting to share its transformative effects with as many people as possible.

After beginning my journey, from the start, I knew in my bones that I wanted to train others. With this newfound assertion, as I had never been so bold before, I asked my trainer at the time for David Grand's cell phone number. It was Tuesday when I first called him because I found out, again, the person shall remain nameless, that David would be available the upcoming weekend. Once I called him that Tuesday, and he answered the phone, he had heard of me from other people.

To recall the phone call: "Hello, Dr. Grand. This is Cherie Lindberg. You know, maybe you've heard of me. I'm one of the founders of the Midwest Brainspotting Institute, and I was wondering if I could take you out to lunch this weekend." He goes, "Are you in New York?" I said, "No, but I can be." He goes, "You're gonna fly in just to take me to lunch?"

Yes, that's how much I needed to meet this man.

We arranged for him to pick me and another brainspotting practitioner up from the airport in a few days. When the day arrived, he picked us up and took us to Long Island, where we walked on the beach, talked, and dreamed about the future of brainspotting. That's when he welcomed me to the team and told me I would shadow the trainers for the next few years to learn more about brainspotting. He gave me a silver pointer to commemorate the moment.

I followed other trainers for years before attending an official training in 2014, where David trained a group of us at his New York City office. Later that same year, I participated in his first international training in Brazil, which included attendees from Japan. While we weren't the first trainers, this was the first time he had conducted training for a group of international trainers. Participants came from as far as England, Scotland, Brazil, and Japan, as well as from within the US, including Colorado and Wisconsin.

That's where he trained us for three days on brainspotting, Phase 1. It was the first time I'd been to New York, and it was a totally new world. A significant cultural reset or initiation, what have you, was when we were walking through Manhattan, and a rat the size of a dog hopped over my foot and went into the sewer. I screamed so loud. I literally thought it was a dog. Once I realized it was a rat, it freaked me out. Its body barely fit into the sewer...ew!

Regardless of rats, shortly after that, I planned to present at our first conference in Brazil in 2016. Between traveling and training, I needed to step back from my clinic—it was becoming too hard to manage a clinic with all this new training and new life pathways that were opening up before me. Before I closed the group practice, I told the staff I would help them learn how to open their own businesses. Then, if they wanted, we could just merge into a loose group. About four people stayed, and we became just that, a loose group. We did this for a couple of years. But within two years of this loose affair, I decided I wanted to be a solo practitioner.

My career and life have always been an evolutionary process involving a lot of adjustment and change. To some, looking in, it could be seen as chaotic or having too much change, and I have often heard this from others. However, the so-called chaotic energy they claim to see, I see as creative evolution. It all depends on who tells the story and how we paint it for ourselves.

When people started negating a journey that I found positive and fulfilling, personally and professionally, I had to let them go. I can't have anyone in my inner circle who sees what I'm doing as chaotic because it becomes clear they are not in the growth energy I aim to be. They're not ready for the growth and the creativity. That's okay. I'm not judging them; I just can't take care of them or absorb any negative energy coming from them.

My lived experience has been that many people struggle with too much change because it can feel overwhelming, destabilizing, and unpredictable. When life shifts rapidly, through relationships, career, health, or inner growth, it can activate fear, anxiety, and a sense of loss.

Our nervous systems crave safety and familiarity, so change often feels like a threat rather than an opportunity. Yet, in order to evolve, we must be willing to let go of the old, to release what no longer serves us, in order to make room for the new. Though uncomfortable, this process creates space for deeper alignment, transformation, and a more authentic life. With compassion, support, and grounding, change becomes not just bearable but a powerful path to healing and growth.

It cracks me up because I talk about this, and people are so sure they have a growth mindset. Yeah, yeah, yeah, I'm in a growth mindset. But, they often don't understand how you apply it daily, as you catch the old mindset or behavior and switch it to the new mindset and behavior.

For instance, I know I don't always have a growth mindset. That isn't the problem. I'm human. I'm not perfect and can get into a destructive mindset, but I catch it pretty quickly now, after years of practice. The primary separation is maintaining a growth mindset and not realizing those slips and changes as growth opportunities. I shift my mindset, and this is what I teach others to do as well. Growth is based on routines and habits. However, it is not easy, and not everybody wants to work that hard at these skills. If you want change, you must build and apply new daily habits. Daily embodiment practices/habits that help shift your body and mind are the ticket to your growth and healing.

Brainspotting is a significant aspect of what I teach to aid in the process of embodiment mindset practices and beyond. It also helps activate a learned and earned attachment, which helps reshape your brain and your belief systems. Brainspotting is moving into the neuro-experiential model of healing and expansion, opening people up to their true essence beyond cultural norms, programming, and the true essence of their spirit. In the words of David Grand, "The neuro-experimental model is open and looks for Indigenous wisdom." Meaning we look for it. We bring it in. We don't want to limit our experience to the Western lens anymore. The genius of the subcortical brain is something to behold, as it represents an expansive model of healing.

When we hold the space for the client, it's whatever is emerging for that client during the brainspotting process. What I've noticed over time, as a practitioner, is that we hold the space so they can heal their trauma and deprogram their conditioning from their culture, society, and generational patterns. Only then do sessions move into expanded creativity, spirituality, intuition, and expansiveness of who they truly are.

Brainspotting, in many ways, serves as a portal to different forms of universal knowledge. When I first meet people, the process feels very cognitive and logical. But as we spend more time together, their healing becomes expansive, shaped by whatever emerges from the neuro-experiential processing with the client. We go into places they can't explain, and I can't explain either.

Each moment is unique. For instance, during sessions, loved ones who have passed away may appear, and memories of them can resurface. Sometimes, their scent lingers, even though they are no longer physically present. Truly inexplicable things. Sessions with clients begin to shift into spirituality, intuition, and the expansiveness of who they are, their real essence, and what they're here on earth to do. While sessions may start out very therapeutic, cognitive, and logical, over time, in the safe space created, clients often begin to explore spirituality and intuition much more deeply.

In one instance, I was working with a woman who had experienced a stillbirth. We spent time processing her grief and healing from that loss when the energy of her baby entered the room. She could feel it. She spoke to the baby, allowing her to say goodbye in a way that brought deep healing to her heart.

In another case, I worked with a mother whose son had been murdered. As we focused on her healing, his presence was felt during our session. She was able to have a conversation with him, express her love, and say goodbye, reassuring herself that they would be together again.

I have even used brainspotting with people facing terminal illnesses, those who know they are dying. Some have profound spiritual experiences, even speaking with Jesus and relatives who have already passed. Skeptics rush to dismiss these moments as imagination or performance, but the experience is deeply embodied. It takes on another dimension when people go through it.

When you're fully present with a client, practitioners often find themselves channeling in ways that can be unsettling, even to us as practitioners. Some practitioners tell me they can physically feel what their clients are experiencing in their bodies, and it can be a startling, almost surreal experience.

I know it freaks me out because, when it first started happening to me, I would know what a client was about to say right before they'd say it. Or, I'd be so attuned that I could physically feel what was happening in their body—only for them to confirm, moments later, that they were experiencing exactly that.

Some might call this attunement, empathy, or heightened sensitivity— terms that feel "safe" and socially acceptable. But to say we're channeling? That takes it to another level, a so-called "woo-woo" space, and that makes people uncomfortable. This is a complex topic to discuss because, although it's happening in offices and practices beyond my own, practitioners are often afraid to talk about it. Fear of societal norms and the pressure to stay within the boundaries of what is considered "normal."

The entire issue has become politicized because we exist within rigid systems that dictate how healing should be done. As professionals, we are told, "This is your box as a therapist, and this is the only acceptable way to practice."

Step outside of that box, and you risk losing your license. But there's a disconnect between what we are taught in graduate programs, what is considered professionally and socially acceptable, and what actually helps people heal. This does a disservice to clients because instead of genuinely listening to them, we impose a prescribed method of healing.

Brainspotting does the opposite; it allows us to be fully present and listen. And yet, when we talk about psychedelics or Peruvian practices, those conversations are becoming more mainstream, more "acceptable." So, with enough power and popularity, could the so-called "woo-woo" aspects of brainspotting also be acknowledged as authentic and valid? Time will tell.

What Can Brainspotting Do for You and Your Clients?

What does brainspotting do? Simply put, it wakes you up. It is all about healing and repairing developmental attachment. The brain begins to reorganize with new information, becoming more integrated and balanced—everything starts to open up, both spiritually and creatively.

Concepts in Brainspotting

We begin with **dual attunement**. The dual attunement frame is where we are relationally attuned to the client, and we, as the practitioners, are attuned to their neurobiology. We're watching what happens as we're holding the space. The client's lived experience, encompassing everything they are, where they have come from, and their lineage, is the frame they bring into the room. We hold that frame relationally and neurobiologically with the client. The therapist also has their own frame and syncs up with the client's. The two frames come together, and we hold them and see where the processing goes. We create a biofield of energy in the holding space with the client. In brainspotting, we access a system inside yourself that works independently; instinctually, the subcortical brain wants to heal and takes us on this journey.

This journey is rarely linear, varying from one individual's experience to another. That's why David calls it the neuro-experiential; it's very neurological and experiential. It rises out of the client's physiology, which represents everything inside a client—that the practitioner holds with them relationally and neurobiologically.

We have another key concept in brainspotting called **uncertainty**. As practitioners, we sit in a state of uncertainty with no assumptions because how can we possibly know what's going on in that client's brain? With 1-4 quadrillion connections, there is no way we can know. After we have begun the brainspotting experience, the client undergoes a neuro-experiential experience, which is a neurologically conscious experience of the brain and body receiving new information. The brain then begins to self-organize around the new information, much like an upgrade. This is how people start to change, grow, and shift.

Limbic countertransference is the next concept within brainspotting. The concept applies to practitioners because if we aren't clearing our emotional baggage out daily, the stuff accumulates from being exposed to our clients' trauma material. Research from the Venice Family Clinic reports, "Vicarious trauma and secondary trauma are both forms of indirect trauma that clinicians experience when hearing the stories and treating the suffering of patients who have experienced trauma. Secondary trauma may occur suddenly, after hearing a patient's story one time; whereas, vicarious trauma represents a shift in the clinician's attitude and worldview after prolonged exposure to patients' suffering" (Venice Family Clinic).

As a practitioner, your past, your vicarious trauma, and your secondary exposure (trauma) will inevitably leak out onto the client or your loved ones. Practitioners must be as grounded and clear-minded as we can. But as we listen to this trauma material, our brains and bodies can absorb the client's trauma material. Our physiology holds onto these feelings; sometimes, that baggage, that vicarious trauma, gets stuck there. It is our responsibility to clear that out so we stay grounded. If not, a triggered therapist is going to intervene more quickly. A triggered healer will intervene and may stop the process out of fear, hindering the client's ability to go where they need to go.

As a practitioner, self-reflection is imperative. We need to make sure we are mindfully communicating without projection or overreaction. WAIT is an acronym brainspotting practitioners use to remind ourselves, "Why Am I Talking?" We want to stay out of the client's process as much as possible and let the client's brain and body do the work.

Holding Space for Clients and Practitioners on the Journey

There is a vast brainspotting community that is branching out now. Heather Corbet and I are building a vast spirituality and intuition community as part of that growth, the Soul Flow Membership Community. We even have a class called "Brainspotting, Spirituality, Intuition, + Manifesting." Most of our attendees are also drawn to these classes because brainspotting has opened them up to having more spiritual and intuitive experiences. Practitioners are asking for support. Maintaining this sort of support network and community is essential.

We all long for community, from your clients to even you as a practitioner. Everybody longs for a deep connection so they can be free to be themselves, but they are also scared. They are scared of the prejudices people have. They are scared of not being accepted. They are scared of being judged. We are all at different stages of growth in this community. Many of us have parts at different stages of healing. This community is committed to welcoming all to have folks come as you are.

We understand that judging others is a phenomenon of our culture. It's just a matter of finding your people. That is what building a community is, despite the paradox of judgment.

Picture this: you're sitting in your office, and a deceased baby appears, communicating with its parent. I've worked with death doulas who describe how spirits come into the room during their work. These ideas may seem foreign to many, and society often responds to the unfamiliar with fear and the othering of those who experience it. Yet, despite spending my entire career in academia, grounded deeply and firmly in logic and research, I've encountered these moments firsthand. I cannot now deny them because they seem inexplicable.

People listen to academics. If you have initials after your name, they'll listen to you. It's unfortunate but true. That journey is not unique. Many people at the beginning of their careers and practices covet their skills and findings out of fear of repercussions from society and within the field. That's where discernment comes into it.

Through Brené Brown's ideas, I learned that I want to live wholeheartedly. She really emphasizes this ideology; her guideposts for wholehearted living are available through her website. To live wholeheartedly, one must be open to pain, rejection, and betrayal as well as joy and love. Even though there is a possibility of displeasure or betrayal, I put my trust in the universe, the people I meet, and my journey here (Brown, 2010).

When I have what looks to some like a bad ending—when my group spoke about me behind my back—I keep all of this in mind. In that situation, I grieved that I couldn't control the other side of the equation, the other narrative of me, because that is not who I am; that's just how I was perceived. After the woman had spoken up, I realized the perception had come from within her. Everyone sees things through a specific set of glasses, and she doesn't have the skills to navigate conflict and stay connected. This, in a nutshell, is usually why relationships break up.

So, I don't have all the answers. I certainly don't, but I'm willing to have difficult conversations with everyone around me. The key to that process is communicating about it, as in, don't let me be the last to hear about myself. Not everyone can align with their values. Many are on autopilot, doing what they have learned for generations. It takes self-reflection and consciousness to do things differently from your programming.

For example, if there's something that has happened where I have triggered you, I hope you will come and talk to me about it. I mentor and teach others a dialogue process so we can navigate conflict, stay connected, grow, and change together. Many believe having hard conversations is too much for them. If I approach somebody and try to have a difficult conversation, they will often assume I'm just trying to shame or blame them. In reality, self-reflection and communication are at the core of success for both practitioner and client.

My Journey with Community

I mentioned earlier how I lost my family when I was young, and on top of that, I was very spiritual as a child. I was labeled the weirdo. To shut all that down, I removed myself socially, apart from a few good friends. In turn, I have always sought a large community, whether through a large family or otherwise. Throughout my youth, up until the last decade, I've taken the risk of building a community again. I kept quiet about everything I knew until I got all my degrees, and then, somehow, it felt safe to come out and be my true self again.

As I mentioned earlier, everyone is at a different stage of personal development, and we live in a society that is often rooted in blame and shame. Not everyone has the same skills and abilities to navigate conflict or to grow in consciousness. Some people immediately go into defense mode, blaming, shaming, or pointing fingers, rather than processing what's actually happening. They are unaware they are on automatic pilot or under the influence of their programming.

When we get triggered, consider it an opportunity to reflect, access, and heal an old wound in real time. It will take us staying conscious of our triggers and reflecting on their origins so we can understand why we're reacting. Healing requires compassion and curiosity. We need someone to hold space for us in a way that fosters understanding, safety, and growth. If you're with someone who lacks self-awareness and struggles to manage their own triggers, the environment is no longer compassionate; it becomes reactive.

This is why so many friendships and relationships fall apart during conflict: people simply don't know how to navigate it. Maintaining a community can be challenging because when we don't feel safe or trust each other, our defenses kick in, making the connection even harder. That's why community is essential, not just for clients but for practitioners as well. It's crucial for both professional success and deep, meaningful healing.

Brainspotting Routines and Practices

Once you practice these techniques, the applications are seemingly endless. Here are a few ways I integrate brainspotting into my regular routine.

Intentional Daily Process

About 40 minutes before I connect with a client, have an appointment, or training, I go into my office and put on the bilateral music. This helps my amygdala to calm down, allowing me to become embodied. It can also be described as self-spotting. I do this process of holding my gaze on a brain spot every day for about 15 minutes. I hold my attention on this spot each morning to feel better connected to my spiritual self. Typically, the space holds my body where I feel calm and at ease.

In my office, I have a window and several paintings. I call them portals, where I know I can look, and they connect me to Spirit, help me get into the flow, and reinforce and anchor my intentions for the day. For some reason, my physiology in these certain spots relaxes, and my creativity begins to blossom.

Then I say a little prayer: "Jesus, son of Joseph, Jesus, son of Mary, Jesus, son of man, Jesus, son of God, ground the divine in my body, let me be a divine instrument for the clients that I'm seeing today and guide me." I'm touching my third eye and my heart to ask for guidance. I have learned to call in the Earth Mother and other elements as well.

During these 15 minutes, I visualize my clients that day, attendees at a training, or I might focus on a marketing idea. Each day is different. No matter what comes to mind, I always keep my journal nearby to write down my takeaways.

Finally, I'll pull a card with a healing message while my bilateral music plays. Sometimes, it's an affirmation card with a simple yet meaningful quote, like, "Release what's no longer needed." In those moments, I take it in and reflect on it. Anchoring in any positive sensations my body is experiencing. Other times, the card contains a deeper healing message, which I read and absorb as part of the process. When I'm doing creative work with another practitioner, the bilateral music is on because I think it taps into the genius of our subcortical brain. Here, I get focused and into a flow state, and beautiful ideas start appearing.

Oils, Crystals, and Symbols

Aside from my painting portals, there are other materials I like to utilize in this process, one of which is essential oils. I put a few oils on myself, and feel like I'm ready for my day.

Best oils to check out? I go through cycles. I've been using the Young Living brand— Freedom & One Heart.

I go through cycles, and right now, I'm really into Young Living's Freedom and One Heart essential oils. Freedom's bottle has a horse galloping, which I love because I love horses. I have a painting in my office of horses galloping called "Into the Light." When I saw the Freedom oil, it resonated with me because that's exactly what I want—freedom. Since I bought the essential oil, I've been using it every day.

One Heart is for unity and community. I also have oils called Love and Protection. My husband may start hacking as soon as he walks into my office. My son comments on how the room smells whenever he walks in, but I love the smells of essential oils.

I also have specific stones and crystals on my desk, which I often hold while supporting someone in my coaching. Some of these stones are from Machu Picchu, and others from Peru with specific energies attached to them. I have displayed them on my desk as they are an essential part of my space.

Symbols are also a big part of my life. I have an infinity symbol tattooed on my arm that reads, "I am Love and Light." When I'm holding space for people who are struggling, I say, "Love," inside my head, "love and light, dear soul, love and light, dear soul." I also have a Flower of Life, which is sacred geometry. Symbols, routines, rituals, and intentionality all speak to me and give me the energy to do what I'm here to do.

Intention Setting and Planning

Aside from my daily practices, I use Self-Spotting Intensives for business planning. I set aside an entire weekend with no clients, nothing scheduled on Friday, Saturday, or Sunday. I put on bilateral music and create an outline and intentions for the year ahead of what I want to see come to fruition.

For example, in 2025, I knew I wanted to take another trip to Peru. I also knew I would be going to Costa Rica to do more work with the Peruvian healing brothers, so I wrote that down. I set an intention to hold at least two trainings a month, and that is happening. I also want to do more healing work on my property. I've planned an intensive for June 2025 that will take place on my property, which I feel strongly about moving forward with.

For 2026, I already know it will be a reflection year. I plan to journal after every major occasion or event, personal and professional, to see how I feel. My intuition is telling me I need to do something different—like letting some things go in 2026. I don't know what 2026 will bring, but I sense that something is shifting. Spirit is telling me this, I feel it in and around my body, though I have no words for it yet. I'm simply reflecting and trying to be honest with myself.

Parts Work

Brainspotting as a Parts Approach

When we think about healing and personal growth, we often focus on the mind and emotions, but what about our physical qualities? Through this chapter, we'll explore how brainspotting, a powerful therapeutic approach, works through the lens of parts-based healing and, in turn, how that connects to the body.

Brainspotting isn't about resolving surface-level symptoms; it's a far deeper process that reveals hidden parts of ourselves holding traumas, memories, and unprocessed emotions. Whether it's the inner child who didn't get the love and care they needed or the protective parts we've created to survive, understanding these aspects of our mind and body is crucial to understanding who we are and how to fully relate to others.

Most folks don't realize that brainspotting is a parts-based approach. When the client focuses on the pointer or "spot," they're working through an issue that bothers them. Different thoughts and sensations emerge. They begin to process their developmental history, and the brain uncovers areas that need reorganization. Afterward, you can just flow through it right then and there. In parts work, you can expect to process memories, thoughts, body sensations, experiences, and even the beliefs you hold.

Many folks can easily flow through their parts; they move through them quickly, their brain efficiently reorganizing and reframing the part. While second nature for some, that ease certainly does not come naturally for everyone. If brainspotting doesn't immediately work for you, it does not mean you are broken. You may just have had more complexity in your development.

For example, you might be like me and have complex PTSD. Simply put, this is when trauma has been repetitive in someone's life. Of course, brainspotting is going to look different for someone who has dealt with repetitive trauma; it has a significant impact on your development, and that's not any fault of your own.

For me, my trauma occurred repeatedly from a very young age, all the way up until I was about 18. When trauma is recurring, especially during those critical brain development stages, parts of you can become stuck in arrested development. Arrested development means certain parts of you remain at the age where your needs weren't met. Unmet childhood needs do not go away. Instead, they often manifest as issues in adulthood.

One time, during a personal brainspotting session, I saw myself as an eight-year-old. My younger self began talking directly to me, and I started to respond to her, listening to her story, full of grief, longing, and the need for validation. In that session, I gave myself what I hadn't received as a child: nurturing myself from within, finally meeting the needs of the eight-year-old girl inside me. Only then did more profound truths reveal themselves.

Having your most adult part compassionately nurture your younger self inside helps you finally know that you are good enough. You are lovable, no matter what you've been told in the past. That was then, and this is now. You just need to keep moving forward! For someone with a complex trauma system, you may need to directly engage with these parts of yourself. I dialogue with my parts even today.

During a session, if you have an eight-year-old inside, we may explore whether you can introduce yourself to this eight-year-old version of yourself. We have you begin to build a relationship with her just by saying, "Hey, sweetheart, tell me your story." Simply by listening, you'll notice the child within you begins to soften. At this point, you might be able to flow with it, or we might need to do a little more work. We may need to retrieve that child, remove them from the abusive situation, and bring them into the present with you. I remember one time, my younger self and I ended up doing the Macarena together!

If you have complex PTSD, a therapist may need to be more involved. While the process may be simple, it can be overwhelming. Healers, coaches, and therapists can guide you through more complex aspects of trauma experiences and layers of arrested development.

In parts processing with brainspotting, I focus on observing and attuning to what's emerging in the moment. Your system will communicate its needs, but you have to be deeply attuned to hear them. That's where I come in to help!

For example, during a brainspotting session, a client might feel stuck and say, "This part's not moving, I need your help, Cherie!" In response, I offer my clients various options. I might present them with a "menu" of ideas or suggest creative ways they might use to move forward. I'm essentially planting a seed and seeing if their system will take it in and if it will help their system shift. They go inside with the suggestions and see what happens. I aim to do as little as possible and stay out of the process because I want the work to come from you, not from me. Your system might just need a couple of seeds to flow!

Often, when people say they want to heal, one part of them genuinely wants to heal, while another part may block the healing process. Why? Because healing requires letting go of things, and that can be scary. People often don't realize that healing frequently involves releasing what's familiar, even if that's a harmful pattern. It can feel like a loss, and grief often accompanies letting go, despite the fact it no longer serves you. You might experience an identity crisis at first, not knowing who you are without that old pattern, which threatens to keep you stuck.

I've seen it over and over again: when people *truly* heal, their lives change. You might lose relationships, change jobs, or shed things that no longer align with who you're becoming. Healing is transformative and beautiful to witness, but it can also be a daunting experience. Any kind of loss inevitably comes with grief. Many people chase the blissful state they envision healing will bring. They want to expand and move forward, but you can't truly heal without letting go of the anchors that weigh you down.

I grew up on the south side of Chicago, where fear was a weapon. The advice I received was simple: "Always look pissed off, don't ever make eye contact, and people will leave you alone." It wasn't the most nurturing environment, to say the least. I didn't realize it at the time, but I began doing my own personal work in my early 20s. This resurfaced later when I began brainspotting.

During that time, I was using April Steele's *Imaginal Nurturing* CDs. I remember one of them saying, "I'm so glad you're here" (Steele). The voice behind those words reflected that warmth. I had a strong reaction to that, wondering, "What's this mamby-pamby stuff about?" Despite my reservations, I was lucky enough to have enough self-awareness to reflect on my reaction. I committed to listening to that CD three times a week for three months!

Initially, I started with a lot of negative thoughts. I thought I might be wasting my time, and some of the concepts honestly sounded ridiculous to me. I didn't realize it at the time, but this was my defense mechanisms; my walls were going up.

When all of a sudden, Glenda the Good Witch, yes, from *The Wizard of Oz*, morphed into my brain, holding baby Cherie. I watched as she gazed into my infant self's eyes and softly said, "You are so precious."

She called me beautiful and bright. I remember feeling something behind my eyes. I didn't understand it at the time, but I didn't stop. I kept doing this, and each time, I felt myself soften inside.

One day, when I was about to quit this silly nonsense, I became Glenda. Eventually, I was the one nursing little Cherie. Initially, I was taken aback by this. But shortly after, in brainspotting, my parts began to show up, and I realized I was reorganizing my development from the inside. I started to love myself more, realizing that I should have been telling myself these things all along: that I was precious, beautiful, and amazing. Miraculously, I was reparenting myself with the help of brainspotting.

I had always had a baseline instinct for nurturing, but I didn't grow up with much of it, so I didn't have much to model it after. By imagining Glenda mothering me, I showed myself how to do it until my adult self could step in and take over. Before that, I was very critical of myself, largely because I had so many critical people in my life growing up. This imaginative process softened all of that, and compassion began to fill my system instead. When you experience a lot of trauma in your development, it is often hard to receive nurturing. It is not familiar to your system. Your system had to adapt in protective ways. It can be scary to let the good in.

I realized slowly that I should have been hearing these good things, and that's where the grief came from. I know my mom and dad did the best they could, but they came from trauma as well. I needed to pick up where they left off with love, remembering that they hadn't been nurtured either.

If I could do it, I realized, so could others. I knew I needed to get others trained ASAP I had to go out and teach people! So many individuals, especially those with adverse childhood experiences (ACEs), are often surrounded by negative research. For example, high ACE scores are linked to a greater risk of depression and other mental health issues, with few positive statistics to counteract that.

But by doing internal work, you can develop a secure attachment from the inside; your childhood doesn't have to be a death sentence. You're not irrevocably "messed up" or "not good enough." That simply isn't true.

When I was growing up, school districts were far from trauma-informed. Teachers were often abusive, hitting and pinching students, and nobody thought twice about it. No one stopped to consider *why* a child was acting out. The focus was on controlling, shaming, blaming, and humiliating children. Those with power cared more about control than understanding the underlying causes of the bad behavior.

Not that education's perfect now, but there is much more awareness about trauma and more natural tools available to help. Educators now understand, for the most part, that when kids act out, it's a response to past traumatic experiences. This summer, Heather Corbet and I will have the opportunity to do the first Brainspotting Phase 1 training for schools. It's coming full circle. I get to make an impact in the schools where I was traumatized before.

Early Resources

In elementary school, I understood something was "wrong" with how my brain functioned, but I didn't know what that was. Later, in grad school, I got into an argument with one of my professors about whether IQ is fixed. He kept asking how I was so certain that IQ could change. When my IQ jumped 20 points after doing EMDR treatment, I knew for sure!

A game-changing resource, Dan Siegel's book, *The Developing Mind,* explores attachment, trauma, and the brain's structure (Siegel, 1999). After this title, I followed Dan Siegel's work everywhere, exploring how relationships influence the brain and energy and information flow through our central nervous system. I deeply resonated with his ideas because it was exactly what I had been trying to convey to others. Of course, I didn't have grants or the ability to conduct research myself, and I had just finished grad school, but with this resource in hand, I had the confidence to stand by my beliefs. In my final semester of grad school, I bought a copy of his book for every one of my professors as validation for some of the experiences I'd shared.

Then, I discovered Allan Schore's work around regulation theory, rooted in developmental neuroscience and psychoanalysis, that explores how physiology actually changes and adapts to trauma. Schore's work validates a lot of my early childhood issues by confirming the very real impact trauma has on our early selves; it can completely reshape us. I couldn't deny the damage anymore, and other professionals have backed up his work as well. (Schore, 2021)

Another one of my favorite researchers, Bessel van der Kolk, expands on how trauma changes us. *The Body Keeps the Score* explores how the physical body bears the burden of trauma, meaning it can sense problems long before we consciously become aware of them. "Trauma interferes with the brain circuits that involve focusing, flexibility, and being able to stay in emotional control. A constant sense of danger and helplessness promotes the continuous secretion of stress hormones, which wreaks havoc with the immune system and the functioning of the body's organs" (Kolk, 2014)

Now, we're in the decade of the brain-body connection, and everyone pretty much agrees there's something to it. Yet there are still professionals who avoid talking about the body. The truth is, we sense things long before we have any conscious awareness. Our bodies play a crucial role in shaping the rest of our brains. The neocortex, which processes higher-level thinking and knowledge, is the last part of the brain to develop. Information comes to us first through our periphery and our bodies, and only later does it form a coherent story in our minds.

Building on the understanding of embedded trauma in the body, Stephen Porges' *The Polyvagal Theory* offers a crucial physiological framework (Porges, 2011). His research explains how the autonomic nervous system, particularly the vagus nerve, influences our response to stress, danger, and safety. The nervous system constantly scans for cues of threat or safety using a subconscious process known as neuroception. Our bodies enter three physiological states based on what they detect: ventral vagal (safe, social), sympathetic (mobilized, fight/flight), and dorsal vagal (shutdown, freeze). Trauma can cause our nervous systems to remain in survival mode, even in the absence of an immediate threat, and talk therapy alone doesn't always fully heal someone or help solve their problem.

This means, conclusively, that we can pick up on things before we have concrete evidence. Ever had the feeling that something was wrong, before you knew what it was? Most of us recognize that sinking feeling in the stomach when something just isn't right. Some people call it intuition, which we'll explore further. Whatever you call it, we've often been conditioned to dismiss it. Porges' work demonstrates that healing must include assisting the nervous system in re-establishing a sense of safety, not just cognitively, but physiologically. Highly effective trauma recovery techniques include breathwork, body-based therapies, and safe relational connection.

Although it's becoming more common to talk about the brain and prove things through the Western medical model, if we can prove something through science, we often validate it as truth. We must remember that there are many things we don't see that are just as true.

Concepts in theoretical physics, like energy, can't always be proven, but that doesn't make them any less real. While we still have a long way to go, data is being gathered and progress is being made. Science is slowly but surely catching up with these sorts of understandings.

_____

What is Parts Work?

So, what exactly is this parts work I've been referencing? Let's unpack that before moving further. The idea is that our bodies are made up of countless parts that work both together and independently. What makes it especially interesting, therapeutically, is the variety of theories about how these parts function. Personally, I view it through the lens of brainspotting when I think about parts work.

In brainspotting, our "lenses" are formed by different parts of our systems.

Our brains function in much the same way. Parts of ourselves hold beliefs, images, and various sensations. Sometimes, these parts show up in the form of trauma and sometimes in spiritual forms. All these aspects of who we are can be separated, meaning our actual, authentic self isn't fully moving forward. We spend much of our lives being conditioned to survive, only to eventually wake up and realize we don't know who we are. That's when we begin the work of retrieving and remembering ourselves. Who are you? This is what I mean when I talk about retrieving aspects of ourselves.

For example, I'm a people pleaser. I spent much of my life fawning over the adults around me, overperforming so they would be happy with me. This still happens today, but I now recognize that it stems from a deep-seated fear of disappointing anyone. I don't want to hurt anyone's feelings, so I often sacrifice myself, as that's what I've been conditioned to do since childhood. It can be easy to slip back into those patterns if I'm not careful.

It's a survival adaptation from childhood, conditioned to help me navigate the environment I grew up in. As adults, our systems will continue to operate in the same way unless we undertake the internal work to update our programming. We must learn to do things differently and to be more intentional, conscious, and mindful of creating healthier habits. We owe it to ourselves to learn and understand how the body and spirit evolve.

Antonio Damasio talks about our deep mid-brain as the home of our spirituality, creativity, and the seat of our souls (Damasio 2010). When we do brainspotting, we access that place in the brain. Yet, with all the programming and conditioning from our culture, we're conditioned and programmed out of who we truly are. From the beginning of our lives, we're just trying to belong and survive. It can be jarring to realize you don't know who you are, but that is already further than most folks get. But you *can* pull yourself out of it. As soon as you honestly ask yourself who you are, you can start doing the work to remember yourself.

Deep Healing Work: Visiting Ecuador

In 2013, I traveled to Ecuador for an intensive with David Grand, as I've mentioned previously. I wanted to remain anonymous, and I figured no one could get into my business if I didn't understand the language. How could I have any conversations? My full intention was to hide, but this experience turned out to be incredibly powerful. Here, in the place I thought I couldn't understand the language, things began to overlap with intuition and spirituality, marking the beginning of reopening a door I had closed off as a child.

During the process, I heard a voice say, "You can transmute the energy in an entire room."

Oh really? Ok then, I asked to be shown how to do that. As soon as I asked, suddenly, these large, flowing white beings appeared behind all the women in the room. A light entered my chest, and I leaned back, overwhelmed by the power of it. That's when I began to speak my mind aloud to the group.

I don't remember everything I said, but I do remember knowing that this world is an illusion. Luckily, there was a translator, and a couple of us were the only ones who spoke English. When I came back to the present moment, David had a Sandy Hook plastic bracelet honoring the victims of the tragedy, and on it, there was the name "Noah," the name of my youngest son. That had been where I focused and was my brainspot. I remember thinking, I want that bracelet. But it was David's, and I was not going to ask. What a bizarre thing to do!

That was the first time I'd seen these beings, but from then forward, I saw them often. Whether in a training, demonstration, or an in-office healing, I honestly couldn't believe this stuff was appearing to me; I thought people were going to think I was cuckoo for Cocoa Puffs. I started channeling, and both spirits and ancestors began entering the room. I didn't understand what was happening, and even at the end, I thought it was just a vulnerability hangover.

Even afterward, I repressed the experience, dismissing it as unlikely…Until I got on the plane back to return home, I opened my backpack to see the Sandy Hook bracelet staring back at me. I said, "How did you know?" in a text to David, and he just replied with a smiley face.

Early Trauma

I've alluded to having had my fair share of trauma. There was emotional and physical abuse that I grew up with. When my parents separated, my mother's brother would babysit my sister and me. This is when he started sexually abusing me. I was acting out a lot for attention, and he took advantage of that and told me he would tell my parents I was good if I let him do what he wanted.

We already covered some of my upbringing and how you couldn't look at anybody the wrong way. Well, there was also a time and place to be out. I grew up in the kind of area where you go out when the sun is out, and it's light outside, and you run back home when the sun goes down. We knew the dark was dangerous.

I remember, in fifth grade, being in the laundromat with my aunt when a woman ran up, knocking on the door, telling us she had been gang raped. She stumbled in, and I quickly locked the door behind her. My aunt and I helped her back into the bathroom. My aunt went to find a phone and left us. My sister and cousins were there too. I had to stay in the bathroom and comfort this woman. I may have been young, but she really made sure to share all the traumatic details of what happened to her, and I just listened to her story. Looking back, she was in shock, and I believe I went into shock hearing everything she shared.

My parents used to fight a lot, and when they would, there was tons of chaos. It felt like I was the therapist; unfortunately, these experiences prepared me for the situation at the laundromat. I intuitively counseled her, assuring her she was safe. I always handled situations well during crisis time, but I shouldn't have had those skills. I was parentified. I always had to be super responsible in the moment, and would fall apart afterward when I could. Usually, alone.

Growing up, there was a lot of bullying and physical fights among the girls in my school to solve problems. Thankfully, I'm 5'9" with a great evil eye, the kind that reads, "Don't mess with me, I'll kill you." One girl in particular that I remember her bullying me for weeks and following me home. One day she finally threated me, I turned around, looked her dead in the eye, and threatened to go for her "pretty fucking face." Her eyeballs went wide with shock and fear, and she backed up because I looked crazy. I'm sure I looked crazy; that was my intent. She never bothered me again after that. This was not my true nature, but I was managing to survive. My true self is definitely more of a lover than a fighter, but those circumstances brought out the worst in me.

Growing up, the school I attended in Tinley Park, IL, had just ended segregation and was starting to enroll more diverse students. They were from disadvantaged neighborhoods, and I was harassed constantly by some of the male students who were coming in. We ended up moving about 20 minutes south to an upper-class neighborhood, but that wasn't much better. I didn't fit in there either because I didn't have a Porsche or even any car of my own.

Those kids all had fancy cars, as well as access to fancy drugs. Spirit is what saved me. Seeing what drugs and alcohol did to my family growing up, I knew I never wanted anything to do with them. It is incredible to think about, because I could have definitely gone down a much different path. I could have gotten completely messed up, assaulted, hurt, or been in all kinds of terrible circumstances that were all around me.

As a rule follower, I was terrified of all those kinds of things happening to me, just like they did to my friends and family. So, I volunteered to be the designated driver first. I was always watchful, making sure my friends got home okay and things like that. I never put myself in a circumstance where I wasn't with another person or group of people. I just knew to protect myself from early on. I did not realize it at the time, but I was hypervigilant of my environment, and it was this instinct that kept me safe.

There were a lot of pretty terrible babysitters when I was a kid. But one in particular stands out: We called her Fat Cindy. We weren't super nice. And she wasn't exactly quick on her feet, which definitely worked in my favor. One day, I saw her spanking my sister. Instinct just kicked in, and I raced out to the garage, grabbed a plastic bat, and marched right back to put a stop to it. I started to hit her with that plastic bat and told her, loud and clear, to quit hurting my sister. Amazingly, it worked: she backed off and started after me, but she never managed to catch me. Even as a kid, I knew how to protect the people I loved and how to run fast when I needed to.

One summer, while I was away, my sister was left with an abusive babysitter. When I came home, she confided in me about something awful that had happened, but she hadn't told our parents. I decided to handle it myself.

Next time she was hired, I tricked the sitter by telling her my dad would give her an extra ten bucks if she mowed the lawn, then pointed her to the mower. What my dad had actually said to me was, "Cherie, don't use this lawnmower. It will shock you." Oops.

Sure enough, she used it and got shocked. Furious, she came after me and slammed her fist into the glass door, breaking it. I called my parents, and when they arrived, the sitter was finally fired. She bled all over the place, yet the police were never called, and she faced no real consequences.

That absence of accountability echoed something even more painful. The time I talked about my uncle for abusing me. It happened shortly after Oprah had aired a vulnerable episode about her own sexual abuse, triggering memories I had dissociated.

I had just gotten my first period, and the mix of fear, shame, and confusion was overwhelming. I didn't trust that my mother would believe me, since the perpetrator was her brother. So when I told my dad, I made him promise not to tell her.

Six months passed, and I felt guilty for not telling my mom. When I finally told her, she was mad at my dad. I felt bad for getting my dad in trouble, but my mom called my grandmother and cried to her because of all the sexual abuse in the family. Not long after that, my grandmother and I were in the grocery store together, and she tried to convince me that nothing ever happened.

"Now, Cherie," she said, "he was just playing with you and tickling you." Very loudly in the grocery store, I said, "Grandma, if you're thinking him putting his fingers up my vagina was tickling, you must think I don't know what sexual abuse is." I had practically yelled, and she got extremely embarrassed. People looked at us in shock.

That was one of the last times I ever saw my grandma or talked to her about the abuse. She never spoke to me about it again. That is when I lost my other uncle and cousins, too. None of them believed me. I never could understand why my grandfather never tried to reach out to me and ask what happened. One minute, we were visiting weekly, and the next, he didn't see me at all. Why did he not question this big change? As is typical in dysfunctional families, my uncle, who abused me, went to family functions, and I did not. I was the only one not at my grandfather's funeral. The family let the child be scapegoated for an adult's behavior.

It's deeply painful that in many families where sexual abuse occurs, the instinct is often to protect the perpetrator rather than support the victim. As a child, I experienced this betrayal firsthand; the adult was protected, and I was left to carry the weight alone. That experience shaped me in profound ways, leaving me searching for the sense of family I never truly had. Many abuse victims experience this, and it messes with their self-concept. Often, they take on the blame for the abuse, thinking it was their fault. Luckily, this was not me. My parents did believe me. They just did not know what to do about it. I knew I did not do anything to warrant my uncle taking advantage of me like that.

One of the reasons I'm so passionate about sharing healing stories is that I want people to know that they, too, can heal. Another reason I focus on growing and nurturing a conscious, supportive community is that I believe we can choose the people we surround ourselves with, even if we cannot choose our blood relatives. We can create spaces rooted in safety, compassion, and truth, where healing is possible and every person is seen, heard, and valued. This is what is missing in our world today. We are so connected as people. Negativity is reigning supreme right now. We need to reclaim our world.

Parts Work and Brainspotting

When it comes to brainspotting sessions, whatever is emerging for the client is part of the client's lived experience and development. As practitioners, we follow that process. This is called following in the tail of the comet. It's coming out of the client organically, naturally, and openly. At the core of brainspotting, we hold space in what we call a dual attunement frame. So, I'm attuned to my clients' relational needs and to their neurobiology.

I watch their movements, such as swallowing, yawning, and twitching. This is how I know their physiology is processing and that they are in their subcortical brain. I ask them to consider what they are noticing in their body, as this helps them stay in their subcortical brain, where all this beautiful, genius information is. A lot of memories the clients don't even remember, and all of a sudden, they remember because we're so deep in that deeper part of the brain. Brainspotting brings out inner wisdom.

There may be times when we are rescuing the part, listening to the part, befriending it, and helping the client; however, generally, in brainspotting, practitioners will try to stay out of the way as much as possible. We hold space for the client to build a relationship with the part. This is what David calls neuro-experiential. It's very neurological, yet also experiential, as it emerges into the client's awareness from the unconscious. This is where things can get a bit funky and weird. All of a sudden, dead relatives start to show up, or profound revelations, like beginning to realize all the emotional weight they carry. There is a great deal stored in our inner life that we are unaware of. The brainspotting process provides an opportunity to explore the treasures and caves within our psyche.

I once worked with a woman of German descent who suddenly felt as though she were in Auschwitz. It was a deeply unsettling experience for her, and she couldn't understand why her body was reacting that way. Sometimes, there are experiences we can't fully explain, but we still deeply connect with them. Some people might call them "past lives," but now with the study of epigenetics, we know that we carry the memories of our ancestors within us.

Is this what we're tapping into here? Perhaps. We don't have all the answers. However, if you explore Indigenous wisdom, you'll find that this is no surprise, as these traditions regularly work with the energy and memories of ancestors who have passed.

There are many things we can sense but can't see. The body plays a crucial role in developing the rest of our brain. We often sense what's happening before we fully understand it, and it's all about being able to recognize that. We all have moments when we just know something is wrong, even though we can't quite put our finger on what it is. Brainspotting and parts work overlap in this process, as the mind is constantly moving, even if we don't always realize it.

CHÉRIE LINDBERG, PHD

Ultimately, healing is rooted in understanding both the mind and body. We may not always have all the answers, but we have the power to sense, listen, and connect with the deeper parts of ourselves that guide us. Through practices like brainspotting and parts work, we can begin to integrate and validate the parts of us that have been lost, forgotten, or hidden away. As we reconnect with ourselves, we open ourselves up to the possibility of a life lived more authentically.

CHAPTER 5

Spirituality and Intuition

My Experience

I sometimes feel like a baby in diapers when it comes to spiritual things; it's new for me, too, really. I'm still evolving and growing, and I try to be open with my clients about my experiences. While I am certainly not an expert on intuition, I think being open about it is important as I try to move forward. This way, others who might feel equally fearful or uncomfortable about this topic can have someone to resonate with and know that I won't judge their experience, whatever they share.

If my insights can help someone, I want to share them. That's why I created a 'Brainspotting and Spirituality' group on Facebook, a private space where brainspotting practitioners in the same boat can share their thoughts and have a place to express them. Initially, I was a little apprehensive about creating the group, but I suspected it could serve as a good platform for connection.

At first, I was just trying to discern who might be open to spiritual experiences. During one of these moments, I encountered a medium who kept telling me I had gifts. The more I tried to change the subject and focus on supporting her, the more she kept pestering me about my gifts and intuition. She was really enthusiastic about brainspotting.

We ended up attending an intensive in Sedona together two years later, talking about what it would be like to collaborate on creating a brainspotting and Spirituality training. We both were observing the same thing. Brainspotting was opening our clients up to more spiritual and intuitive experiences. Just as everything was picking up, my girlfriend passed away, which really opened the door spiritually for me. I began sharing my experiences with my friend, who had been telling me I had these gifts.

When I was little, I saw spirits, and I would tell people about them. I learned to stop sharing that pretty quickly. My parents would respond by telling me I have an overactive imagination, and my friends thought I was a weirdo. I learned to shut all that down to be accepted. I just wanted to belong. I then became the type of kid to spend all their time focusing on academics so I could legitimize my sense of belonging through education. People tend to listen to you when you have degrees. The great American way. A few degrees and decades later, I'm finally no longer terrified of sharing my experiences. I know my sharing can help others out there.

Early Encounters

Reflecting on my experience with David Grand and the white flowing beings, I started analyzing myself and wondering if I might have some kind of disorder. It felt so surreal, and I couldn't tell if I was hallucinating, dealing with PTSD, or if something else was going on. All I could focus on was David's acceptance of it and playing along with the process; from there, it evolved.

I still don't know if those beings are parts of myself, spirit guides, angels, or ancestors. Everyone has different terminology to explain the inexplicable, whatever they might be called. I call them to me daily now and know they are my helpers. Especially when I'm doing healing work, and it can be... interesting, to say the least.

One instance in Milwaukee stands out particularly.

I was attending a training, and a woman attending had a brother who had been murdered. During the training, she was using a walkie-talkie when I noticed the beings starting to appear. I knew right away that we were about to go deep. At first, I tried to ignore them. I was skeptical and thought maybe my brain was just making things up, but I couldn't ignore what my body was telling me. We were able to go deep in the brainspotting process, and her brother came in during the processing, which helped her get closer to his murder.

I can sense things psychologically, and interestingly, spirits are more present when I'm channeling through my body. For example, I recently consulted with a client who was feeling stuck with a couple of her clients. She spoke about two young girls in particular who were very angry and demanding. I had some intuitive impressions about the girls, so I asked if she would like me to share, and I ended up blowing her mind.

From the description of my client, I wondered if their brother got a lot of attention for being the only boy in the family. As she described working with the brother, I noticed that the brother's process and the girls' process were super similar. I told her that it sounded like those little girls had to be demanding if they wanted to get any attention in the family. That was an "oh my God" moment for my client. She shared more about the little girls, saying, "He always gets his way." As this client, with whom I was consulting, began parallel processing, everything started to fall into place, from the girls' anger to the exhausting nature of the family dynamic.

There's a sacred stillness I enter when I hold space for others. In that place, insights come through effortlessly, like whispers carried on a breeze, entering my body, my mind, my spirit. I don't always share them immediately. I wait, I listen. But when a client asks, "What did you notice during my process?" I speak. And what I share often lands deeply; they feel truly seen, deeply heard, and profoundly understood.

I've come to embrace these intuitive gifts. I'm not just listening with my ears, I'm sensing, receiving, attuning to something greater. Recently, I've been working with a psychic and healer who told me I reminded him of John Holland. That was humbling and affirming, especially coming from someone who walks the path of deep spiritual work himself.

It's becoming clearer: my ability to perceive, feel, and share what moves through me is not only real, it's part of my purpose. It's how I help others find their way back to themselves.

Even though it was very affirming and validating what this medium said to me, I told him that I wasn't sure if I wanted to be that big; I'd rather continue doing small things in secret. I'm already responsible for the lives of many people through the work I do, and I'm not sure I could handle more. I prefer keeping things manageable and behind the scenes, but he told me that I would need to put a system in place over the next two years. He said things like he could see me tripling my income or speaking on stage every night. That definitely freaked me out.

There's a part of me that wonders, "How far can I really go?" I know there's a side of me that has the potential to help more people, but I also have to consider my family, my own life, and my future. I can't say I have all the answers to this journey, but I do know that I'm not alone. Others are experiencing similar things, and I want to share my journey openly.

I can relate to people easily, and I think that's one of the reasons my courses have been so successful. Heather Corbet and I launched a soul-flow group membership online, with a considerable waiting list! It happened overnight.

Many practitioners wanted to explore both their spiritual selves and brainspotting, and it's been amazing to see the high level of interest. We are rebranding this year as "Spirit Code" and are excited to see it grow by hosting an immersive experience at my home in the fall and connecting with other folks open to exploring.

Spirituality goes hand in hand with brainspotting, helping us find a portal into universal knowledge through brainspots that help us access parts of ourselves that we've lost. Through this process, we reconnect with those lost pieces, bringing them back into our lives and becoming who we were truly meant to be. We have the part of ourselves that we show to the outside world, and then we have this inner terrain that we often keep to ourselves.

This work we do as healers is soul work. Inner work. Gently retrieving parts of ourselves that have frozen in earlier chapters of our lives, or even inherited patterns from those who came before us, and welcome them home into the present. This is truly soul retrieval: meeting what was lost or left behind, and weaving it into our wholeness now.

I see my role through this lens. It hasn't always been that way, but as I open further on my own journey, I notice how this approach beautifully echoes the wisdom found in many pathways of healing and coaching. The more I learn and experience, the more I find these universal threads of returning to ourselves, of inviting every part, every story, back into belonging.

I know I'm not alone on this journey. Other healers are going through the same experiences, seeking to tap into the spiritual aspects of their work. Therapists, coaches, healers, and psychologists are all trailblazers in their own right. We've come into this world feeling alienated, often the "weird ones" in our families, the outsiders. We feel things deeply and see what others don't.

Learn more about *Spirt Code*

With compassion and empathy, we're often the ones who struggle to simply "lighten up," a phrase many of us have heard all too often. We tend to do things a little differently, carving out our own path. I truly believe that, because of this, we can rise together and learn from one another.

We are the ones bringing light to the darkness. The bearers of hope to the hopeless. We hold this energy and transmute it. In some instances, I'll be walking one step ahead, sharing what I've learned so that others can follow in my footsteps. Sometimes you'll be sharing expertise only you can offer.

I encourage each of you to walk alongside me. We need as many people as possible to shine their lights out there so that others can find their way home.

Peruvian Practices

Peru has always held a special place in my heart, a land that calls to the soul with its ancient wisdom and sacred traditions. Over the years, I've been fortunate to immerse myself in the richness of its culture, particularly the profound healing traditions. This path is deeply rooted in the art of working with energy, symbols, rituals, and ceremonies, where every element in nature carries meaning and medicine.

In the Andean traditions, animals are more than creatures; they are powerful allies and guides. The snake, for instance, is revered not for its form, but for its essence. As it sheds its skin, it becomes a living metaphor for transformation, release, and transcendence, a reminder that we, too, are capable of letting go and becoming something new. While snakes have never been my favorite animal, I've come to deeply respect their role in the symbolic language of growth.

One such symbol is the *Chakana*, also known as the Andean Cross. While it's commonly understood to represent the four cardinal directions, it also holds a much deeper significance. To those who walk the spiritual path, the Chakana is a portal, a bridge between dimensions, providing insight into the complex and layered nature of existence. The meaning of these symbols evolves as one delves more deeply into the teachings; they are not static, but living, breathing codes that unfold over time.

And then, there is the condor, a creature of breathtaking majesty. In Andean cosmology, the condor is not just a bird, but a sacred messenger, a bridge between the heavens and the earth. It soars above the mountains with grace and power, embodying freedom, spiritual insight, and the strength to rise above life's challenges. The condor invites us to widen our perspective, to see with the eyes of wisdom, and to remember our connection to something far greater than ourselves. I continue my training in these traditions. These teachings continue to shape how I understand healing, transformation, and the sacred journey we are all on.

Exploring the Peruvian worldview has shown me how profoundly it differs from the Western paradigm. In this sacred tradition, everything is energy, alive, interconnected, and deserving of reverence. Central to these beliefs is *Pachamama*, Mother Earth, who is honored not just as a concept, but as a divine presence with whom we are in constant relationship. The *Apus* (sacred mountains) have guides and spirits within that want to support us and share their wisdom.

Energy work in this tradition involves sacred tools, codes, and practices that facilitate healing and transformation. I carry a set of *Chumpi* stones, beautiful, carved healing stones used to clear, shift, and realign energy. Someday on my healing path with the Peruvian traditions, I will learn how to use the *Chumpi* stones for deeper healing. Each one holds a unique frequency. I've also begun learning about being a *khipu* carrier, bundles of initiated stones that become living allies in ceremony and energy medicine. These stones are not passive objects; they are awakened, honored, and activated with sacred intent. They connect to my energy, supporting me to heal others.

Khipu carriers require initiation and energization. My understanding of these ancient traditions is still developing; there is much to learn about working with them, but they are crucial to various Peruvian spiritual practices.

Although I'm still a novice in these ancient ways, I feel incredibly grateful to be walking this path. Every step brings new revelations. There's a depth to Peruvian spiritual practices that invites you to experience life not just with the mind, but with the heart, the body, and the spirit, fully attuned to the wisdom that lives in the land, the animals, the sky, and the stones.

Healing work is such a turbo boost! Intuition also plays a significant role in this process. It comes in through my work with spirits. The spirits often step in to assist during healing. These are just a few of the basic terms and concepts, but the entire practice is extremely complex. What I share here is but a glimpse of some of the practices and tools used around the world. A tiny sample of the deep spiritual ocean available for exploration. There is a lost education out there. Turns out, there are folks out there who think it's perfectly normal to see spirits and work with the dead. I had a lot to learn.

When I first opened my business, 'Get Connected Counseling and Consulting,' I was drawn to the essence of connection, both within ourselves and with the world around us. An intern once joined me for supervision, sharing that my presence reminded her of a wisdom keeper from another era. Over the years, others have told me they catch a glimpse of me in a purple robe, as if seeing a version of me that belongs to a tradition of deep healing and guidance. While I honor these reflections, I know that particular title isn't mine to claim.

Instead, my path has always been one of spiritual growth and respect, especially as I've learned from Peruvian healing traditions and beyond. With every step, I've become more curious about the ways people heal and return to themselves. In my work with brainspotting, I'm often struck by the beautiful parallel: together with my clients, we're inviting home the parts of themselves that were pushed aside or silenced out of necessity, so they could endure challenging chapters of their lives. These parts held a kind of wisdom and protection, helping them to survive.

Now, my role is to guide clients in gently welcoming these lost or hidden aspects back into belonging, helping them reclaim their wholeness, one heartfelt piece at a time.

Getting to Peru

The intern I was supervising suggested that I join the trip to Peru. They were going on the trip because some healer initiates were going to initiate their *Khipus*, and they also wanted to visit Machu Picchu and several churches. My business partner and I decided to go as a way to celebrate our business partnership.

(I should mention here that I've never done any drugs in my life, except for alcohol. Even with that, I barely drink. I've seen the damage alcohol can cause, and I've chosen to include it in my life rarely.)

Once I got to Peru, I studied sacred plant medicine. In particular, I read several books about the ceremonies that center around these practices. *San Pedro*, a cactus leaf boiled down to create a hallucinogenic medicine, especially stood out to me. However, native healers dislike the Spanish term, as it's a colonizer's term from the conquistadors.

The Quechua, an ancient term, refers to this as *Wachuma* or grandfather medicine, as it is a very mild hallucinogen. For five days, we had ceremonies connected to *Wachuma*. After these ceremonies and rituals involving *Wachuma*, I saw faces in the mountains, felt the earth speaking to me throughout the entire experience, and felt deeply spiritually aligned with who I was evolving into. I felt deeply connected to the Earth and the ancient healers who were speaking to me. I absolutely love nature! I felt a deep sense of peace and love for all humanity.

What I didn't love were the events that followed.

One of the leaders from our group had an apprentice who was trying to pursue a married woman. His behavior seemed inappropriate and as though he was grooming her. The Peruvian healer spoke about past lives, claiming that the two of them had been married in another life, which didn't sit well with me. I could understand a connection from a past life, but she was married to someone else in this life, and it wasn't okay to interfere with that through spiritual practices.

They were using the idea of past lives to justify their behavior in the present. I became genuinely concerned that this young woman was being taken advantage of, so I spoke up about it. In response, the healer read the cocoa leaves for me in front of the entire group. He looked at me and said, "You do not believe."

Suddenly, I felt an energy leaving me, and everything became so confusing. Though I had never experienced something like this before, I instinctively looked at him and said, "You do NOT have permission to be inside." I could feel my system shutting down at this point. I did not feel safe and no longer trusted the leader of this group.

After that experience, I thought I was completely done with Peruvian traditions. In my mind, they lacked integrity and acted as if they knew everything, because I'd seen firsthand how manipulative they could be. I decided I wanted nothing to do with it again. I chose to step away from the spiritual route and shut it down…

At least until I met my friend, Teri Nehring.

Tito, Tupac, Wilkapicchu, and Villa Inti Wasi

When I met Teri Nehring, I explained what had happened, and she reassured me that the healing brothers she knew were not like this Peruvian healer I described in my previous experience. It took her three years to convince me to try again. The only reason I finally agreed was that we were in the middle of a brainspotting session, she was holding space for me, and during the session, I found myself back in the land of Machu Picchu in Peru. I sensed that I was meant to bring a group to Peru again. The message was clear: I had to return. Teri also told me, "I've been working with them for over 16 years. They are following a path of integrity and are aligned with what they say."

Tito, Tupac, and their brother, Wilkapicchu, are Peruvian but were visiting Teri in Costa Rica to practice sacred ceremonies and rituals. Truly, gentlemen of integrity, one and all. You can listen to Tito on my podcast. His brother Tupac is well-known in Peru as a spiritual leader. The brothers have complete integrity and a profound love for people, dedicating their lives to healing work and the spiritual path.

Reparative Experience

So, during this trip to Costa Rica in January 2024, I met Tito, Tupac, and Wilkapicchu, meeting up at Teri's retreat center, *Villa Inti Wasi*, which in Quechua is "House of the Sun." Such a beautiful place.

The retreat was attended by a group of people, all of whom were *Khipu* carriers, working with the *Khipu* sacred tools of healing stones and other objects, which can be encoded and activated to facilitate proper healing. I'd fallen out of this practice, having learned a bit about it over a decade earlier. The *Khipu* is connected to a wisdom keeper. There is an energy exchanged between the wisdom keeper and the stones that allows for more profound healing for those they work with.

With the trip to Costa Rica, the theme was: Remembering the Love that we are. The leaders of the retreat taught us about *Munay* and the original *Munay* ceremonies and teachings of love. *Munay* means unconditional love.

It is quite a complicated system. I know bits and pieces of this stuff, though Teri has spent 16 years studying it. I am very much still learning. Essentially, we were learning various methods to identify and shift energy through different ceremonies and rituals. We were learning how to release negative energy and shift into positive energy, specifically love energy, and how to manage our own internal systems to become aware of the kind of energy affecting us. What type of energy is influencing me right now? What is the ceremony or ritual that I need to perform to shift and learn to master my energy? How do I release *Hucha*? (*Hucha* is the negative energy we carry that causes us suffering.)

Often, we would go out in nature and call on the elements: fire, wind, water, and earth. *Pachamama* represents our earth mother, and *Momma Kocha* represents our water mother, including the sea, lakes, and other bodies of water. It is calling in the elements for help. For me, I don't just call on the elements. I also call on the God of my understanding and Jesus with the intention to ground the divine within me. I use these practices to rewire my brain and central nervous system. This helps me become more aware of when I'm triggered and then practice shifting that energy, so I can show up as the most loving human being possible.

On this trip, Tito affirmed that I would become a *Khipu* stone carrier. He basically said that I need to. I wasn't convinced, but after some reflection, it's clear that this was the direction I needed to take. I accepted it, but had no idea what it would look like.

We arranged for me to meet with Tito online. He offered his teachings and read from a book (T'ito, 2018) that he had written to help me prepare. The whole process is very complicated for my brain. I'm studying the original Quechua of the Indigenous people. Some words do not have an exact English equivalent. But the more I practice and work with Tito, the more familiar it feels. There is a saying that I have tried to live by: "A little bit by a little bit." Just a little bit of work each day makes things easier. I have seen things shift already.

I started out really interested in controlling the process to learn everything, understand the language, and live with more joy. I got so overwhelmed and lost. In a recent conversation, he was talking about something, and I came to the realization, "Oh, I already know that…I just learned that the other day."

Then I thought, "Wow. Maybe this is what 'poco poco' means. I think it is getting absorbed in a way that helps me, and I am beginning to understand it finally."

Little bit by little bit.

I wanted to become a stone carrier to remind us that our roots are love: pure love and only that. We must remember who we are and where we come from as human beings, for the sake of humanity. We can't continue to destroy ourselves on autopilot. When we remain on autopilot, we sabotage ourselves. If we tap into our roots, we can reconnect with that love.

There is a great longing in the world for love, belonging, and connection. That is what I want to speak about, and that is what this book, *Sacred Knowing,* is all about.

"Come back, remember yourself. Come back to who you really are."

Everybody who can do that in their own way will be able to heal. I want people to know that they can heal; the wisdom is inside each one of us. I want them to know that their suffering is not in vain. There is a lot you can do to heal, and you don't have to do it alone. Our world is so disconnected and out of relation to each other.

My hope is that by talking about this, by sharing my experiences, more people will move toward the path of healing. There are resources available to help—mentors, coaches, and healers are readily available. I want people, as beautiful individuals on the earth, to gain a new perspective on life. People are disenchanted, we're traumatized, disengaged, cynical. This is why there is violence. We are desensitized, and many no longer feel empathy. Our dark shadow side has taken over.

Our brains are hardwired for the negative because we need to survive. We have not learned our historical lessons. We keep repeating the generational trauma in new forms. We keep reenacting our suffering. This is why we are capable of killing others. People are fed up, and dissociation and calculated impulses to hurt as we hurt have taken over. "You don't care about me, why should I care about you?" It is one result of not listening or connecting to each other.

My husband, Paul, and I studied with the brothers together in the summer of 2024, and what stood out to me was that every time Tito discussed the energies, he could always delve deeper into them, never staying at surface level. When I'm talking with them, it feels like I have ADHD. When the brothers share, they are transmitting and transmuting energy with every word they share. I can feel something happening in my body, but I have no idea what's going on. I start to see and hear things. It's a wild experience.

Brainspotting has a similar effect on me as *Wachuma*. During a session, I can enter a different dimension and experience things my husband has never experienced. In Peru, this time, he decided to go on his own medicine journey and was able to go deep, reclaiming parts of himself he had lost. He has always been very supportive of my healing journey, and is now joining me on the path.

Then some truly lovely healing happened between my husband and me. We've been married for 35 years, and it was amazing to see him let some of his defenses down after all this time. When we revisited the brothers in Costa Rica, we focused on letting love deeper into our hearts.

We've planned to bring another group to meet up in Peru in October 2025. Tito and I have even discussed creating a documentary to help the world awaken to Peru's true essence, so we'll be traveling back with a videographer this time to see what happens.

Life really can take you anywhere, and you never know who you'll meet along the way.

We are spiritual beings having a human experience, one where we're meant to shed the things we no longer need. We do this to move closer to our higher selves and to continue doing what we're meant to do here.

For me, this book is part of that legacy; an opportunity to encourage others to share their experiences and to find a mentor if they, too, wish to follow their curiosity. I want to help people heal themselves and offer solace to those who have faced similar challenges. This path certainly isn't easy, especially if judgmental people surround you, but you must have faith in your process and journey.

In my family, this has opened an opportunity for me to get in touch with and clear transgenerational trauma from my lineage. My hope is that the more I clear this, the less the current generation will need to. They say that there is a carrier in every generation who feels, sees, and moves energetically what the family has not been able to release.

Through Daniel Foor's work with ancestral medicine, I'm beginning to understand a profound truth: it is not solely my responsibility to heal my lineage (Foor, 2017). I'm learning that I can call upon my ancient ancestors, those who have gone before me and already done their own healing work in their lifetimes or beyond. I am not alone in this journey.

For a long time, I unknowingly carried a savior complex. I believed it was up to me, through my suffering and effort, to do all the healing, to ensure that future generations might thrive. But now, I am realizing I have help.

This awareness brings such relief. I am supported. I can call on my well and wise ancestors to walk with me, guide me, and assist me in this lifetime. I'm not the beginning nor the end of this healing path; I'm part of a continuum, and I am held.

History Repeats Itself: A Wake-Up Call

There is something harrowing about watching history repeat itself. When we refuse to reflect and integrate, the same stories play out, with even greater intensity and cost. We say "never again," yet drift quietly toward the very horrors we swore to prevent.

We can walk through life numb, disconnected from ourselves and others, stuck in loops of fear and denial. Empathy fades, and in that emptiness, hatred has space to fester. Instead of honoring our differences, we suppress them and trade truth for control, diversity for uniformity. Instead of embracing diversity as the key to thriving, we're forcing others into conformity, attempting to control perspectives rather than celebrate the richness of differing views.

Those who are silent are frozen; they are afraid, voiceless, and vanishing beneath their own despair. Meanwhile, those gripped by control mask their pain with power, remaining blind to the suffering they inflict. This imbalance feeds itself, a toxic dance in which the compliant enable cruel narcissists to manipulate and inflate the egos of people pleasers.

None of this is a coincidence. But an outward expression of our collective inner fragmentation. Until we heal, together, we remain trapped in the same repeating tragedies of oppression, violence, and human suffering.

Tito speaks of the "Solar Path," an ancient Incan wisdom long buried. It calls us to remember, to rise, and to live from a place of soul instead of survival. That is why I am here; it is my soul mission to reconnect people to a new way. One that's actually quite old, in danger of being forgotten. To share these teachings, ceremonies, and rituals, and support people's soul mission to a higher consciousness. Sounds cheesy, I know.

Your mission, if you choose to accept it…

That is why I told Tito I wanted his help. I craved support to get this information out there, and I asked if there was a way for me to videorecord the group and all of his teachings so we could create a documentary.

The documentary producer and I have known each other for over 10 years. I was in one of his other documentaries, *Light in the Darkness*, about mental health (Murphy, Gartzke, 2019) Shaman Motion Pictures. This is a young filmmaker who wants to make a difference in the world, and I've always supported that. I took him to Ecuador with me years ago, when I first encountered those beings, making it all the more interesting that he's going along on this trip to Peru.

Ancestral Healing at Lake Pomacanchi

During our most recent visit to Peru, the brothers took us to Lake Pomacanchi for a water ceremony to cleanse energy. Locals say water spirits reside there, and *Ausangate*, one of the mountains, is thought to hold a powerful spirit within it.

Once we arrived at the lake, we began the water ceremony, standing in a circle. Suddenly, I was overcome with fear. I have no idea why, but terror gripped me completely. I asked the group to go ahead first while I took a moment. Everyone was staring at me, but I politely requested my space. We stepped into the lake, and I noticed the large eucalyptus branches that they smack you with. The ceremony is accompanied by chanting and drumming, all meant to help shift energy and release what no longer serves you. Eventually, it was my turn to enter the water.

The lake, freezing cold, I internally battled whether I could handle the temperature. I was extremely anxious, but the three brothers were so gentle. We waded into a section of the lake, and they began chanting and smacking the eucalyptus leaves. That was manageable, but when they poured the water over my head, I completely lost it. I started bawling uncontrollably, and it felt like I was drowning. Maybe I had a drowning experience in a past life, or something like that. I know my mother has a deep fear of water, but I still didn't understand why I had such an intense reaction. The brothers assured me that everything was okay.

My poor husband could hear me crying. It's difficult to watch someone go through this, and we were instructed not to face the person who was going through the ceremony, but rather to keep our backs turned. It was an incredibly vulnerable experience. When the ceremony was over, they guided me to the grass, where I collapsed into a fetal position and proceeded to cry for the next 20 minutes. I was completely overwhelmed with the entire experience.

I kept talking to myself on the inside, reassuring myself, "Sweetheart, it's okay. I've got you. Boy, you're so sad, I don't know why you're so sad, but it's okay, you're gonna be okay, I've got you." I just kept repeating this to myself the entire time. Clearly, this was a younger part of me, and my Self was trying to soothe her.

Finally, almost as if a light switch had gone off, something shifted inside of me. I had no idea what any of it was about, but suddenly I felt better. I got dressed, and I felt like a million dollars. This ceremony certainly did move some sort of energy. I remember thinking of my ancestors during this process.

Everyone was asking me what had happened, but I couldn't give them an answer. I truly didn't know. They said it was painful to hear, and I can imagine it was, considering they couldn't actually see me during the ceremony.

This is similar to the healing work we do in brainspotting as well. You follow the process with a therapist supporting you. Then, you enter this uncertain space, intending to heal something, knowing that something internal is shifting, but you don't always understand exactly what it is. We have a saying in brainspotting: "You do not have to know what it is to know that it is."

Six months later, I was working with a Celtic traditional healer to release energy from my great-grandmother. My grandmother passed during the pandemic, and the healer stated that my great-grandmother on my mother's side was earthbound. She carried a dark, negative energy, which is why I've tried to distance myself from her. She, too, was an abuser in the family.

During the session, my grandmother appeared in my mind with a boat full of ancestors. They pulled my great-grandmother into the boat and took her to a place where she could continue her work. She was not well. There are beliefs that the dead continue to grow on the other side. There are also beliefs that some of the dead do not grow and remain unwell. My great-grandmother had not done her work on the other side. By performing this ceremony, we were helping her connect with those on the other side who could assist her.

Paul, my husband, had embedded a *Chicana* from Peru into our fence at our home. I focused on a brainspot while the healer was drumming, and as I did, my brain visualized Tito and Tupac emerge from the *Chicana*, from the fence, and into my yard; Lake Pomacanchi was in my yard. I saw them holding the flute and the drum, and we did another lake ceremony, but this time, I was the one pouring water over my ancestral line. Later, my husband came to me, and I held him as I poured the water over him and my two sons, Zach and Noah. Many healers hope that if they do their work on their path, the next generation will not have to suffer.

My sons, mother, father, sister, and brother were all there. My sister's family and all they are connected to were also there. There was this long line of ancestors, and I couldn't even see some of their faces, but it felt as though we were healing them through the water. It was interesting because going through that ceremony in Peru had been terrifying for me, but doing it with my ancestors brought me a sense of relief. There was a sense of purpose and knowing about it that I can not put into words here.

I watched the ceremony for about half an hour, a profound sense of healing of ancestral energy washing over me. I remember holding my mother, father, children, husband, sister, and brother close as I poured water over their heads, reassuring them that everything was okay. All crying, just as I had, I comforted them as I had comforted myself.

"Let it begin with me."

I often say this to my fellow healers. We have to be the ones to go first because we help others explore the darkest corners of their psyche. We enter the darkness, bring light to it, and say, "This is how you can do it."

We lead by example so that others don't feel so alone. These stories are a testament to how my spirituality has expanded and opened. They are incredibly powerful, and they've helped me heal a great deal. My greatest hope is that they will inspire you to continue on your path or awaken to new possibilities.

I didn't realize there was a part of me holding all this pent-up emotion. Over time, I've noticed I don't have as much anger toward my parents as I once did. What I didn't understand at the time was that the anger I felt toward them connected directly to my ancestors.

There was a younger part of me that wanted a certain kind of mom and dad, but I didn't get it, and it all stemmed from the dysfunction in my grandparents' generation. There is a long line of trauma on both sides of the family. It's an endless cycle for many. I know others find themselves in a similar situation because I've held space for people who feel the same way. My parents' trauma is unhealed, as their parents' trauma was unhealed.

I once had a woman come to one of my training sessions, and she sat down and said, "I don't like my parents or ancestors." She had this attitude that if she didn't like her ancestors, then how could I possibly help her? She was pretty resistant, even cranky about it. I suggested working with the higher selves of her parents and ancestors, and that evoked curiosity. In front of a crowd of 40 people, we began working with her ancestors, parents, and their higher selves. It was extremely vulnerable and beautiful.

Inner wisdom began to emerge for her. All the pain and suffering she had endured traced back to patterns in her ancestry. As we worked through this, her suffering eased, and she experienced a sense of relief. Often, these are one-and-done demos for me, but sometimes people return, and we build a relationship as they go deeper in their training.

In this case, I don't remember her name, and I don't know where she went, but I do know that the brainspotting practices provided her with relief. In my view, these experiences are just as real as conducting a research study and getting approval from a board. We tend to discount these types of experiences in the Western world, but practices like these are entirely normal in Peruvian culture.

David Grand has said, "The neuro-experiential model is looking for ancient wisdom."

And David, we found it. It's already happening. When we reach these deeper places, people can find wisdom. We connect with that subcortical brain, expanding our ability to release and tap into creativity. As people heal and release, they open themselves up to spiritual experiences. I see it all the time, and I'm a living example of it.

Ancient Wisdom Meets Modern Science: The Power of Sound

In tandem with ancient wisdom, modern research is increasingly validating the transformative effects of sound therapy. Practices such as drumming are now being studied for their ability to shift states of consciousness. Scientific exploration into the use of music, mantras, and vibrational frequencies is shedding light on how sound directly influences the central nervous system, offering powerful tools for regulating emotional and physiological states.

These findings affirm what Indigenous cultures have known for centuries: sound is medicine. This isn't a new revelation; it's a long-standing truth that is finally being acknowledged and understood through the lens of science. As research catches up with tradition, more people are awakening to the profound healing potential embedded in these ancient practices.

Truth is, traditional Western medicine is falling short. It no longer helps people heal in the way it once did. It's symptom-based, leaving root causes largely unaddressed.

As a result, more people seek these alternatives. We've only just begun to scratch the surface of the practices and cutting-edge methods that are out there, and I encourage you to explore what other cultures have to offer. There is much to learn.

Celtic Practices

Since my friend Kim passed, there's been a message within me telling me to visit the places I've always wanted to travel. My parents never had the chance to go to these places, but they both dreamed of visiting Scotland. They had accepted that it was something they would never get to do, but I made the decision that I must go.

My husband and I are of Irish and Scottish descent, which made me start to realize the idea of going. I've always loved Celtic music, Celtic knots, and the culture itself, so it felt natural that we should go to Scotland.

There's a shop in Door County, WI, I visit regularly, where I buy Irish wool and llama socks to keep warm each winter in Wisconsin. I adore the clothing, you'll always find me in woolies during winter months!

In 2024, we finally made our way to Scotland. My husband's fifth great-grandfather was buried there, and we set out to find and visit him. In the end, unfortunately, we couldn't locate his gravesite. Regardless, it was incredible to be in such an ancient graveyard, where we knew some ancestors lay, fascinating for both of us.

For Scottish clans, there was a significant event, the Battle of Culloden. It marks the beginning of the British erasing their heritage and squashing any rebellion. When we arrived at the site, we were both overcome with emotion.

The British soldiers had guns, while the Scottish clans still fought with swords, resulting in a brutal massacre. The Scottish clans were slaughtered. Previously, when clan battles ended, women were allowed to enter the battlefield to tend to the wounded and retrieve the dead. But after this battle, the British refused them. Not only did they kill every man, but they stripped the bodies of all their belongings, an act of deep humiliation, leaving them naked on the field. Following the battle, the Gaelic language was banned, and the Scots forcibly displaced to other counties. It was a deeply colonialistic act.

Pre-Scotland Sessions

While in Scotland, we looked for our family crests to trace our heritage. Along the way, we had the opportunity to meet some modern Scots. One of our favorite bands, Skerryvore, performed live. Such a special experience! I'm not sure if it's the lyrics or their accents, but the music is deeply spiritual to me.

During the performance, I was reminded of an experience I had before traveling, connecting with a woman who studied Celtic practices.

She once told me that there would come a day when I would step onto a certain land and feel an undeniable, powerful connection to it. She was right. For me, that place was the Culloden Moor, near Inverness, in the mystical and magical Scottish Highlands.

During a Celtic healing ceremony, I learned that the process was more about allowing than doing. She would connect to my ancestral energy through the steady rhythm of her drumming, then share what she perceived, guiding me to reclaim parts of my soul that had been lost through the experiences of my ancestors.

Over the course of our sessions, she identified recurring themes. One of the strongest was scarcity, particularly the scarcity of money. This came as no surprise, as it has haunted my lineage for generations. She also sensed a deep current of negative maternal energy. These women, my foremothers, had not been protectors of their children. That realization stirred a well of anger within me. I found myself holding a long-standing resentment, unable to fully understand how they could fail to shield their own.

There is a lot of trauma in my ancestral line, it turns out. But having sessions with her from time to time has been incredibly helpful. These sessions have allowed us to uncover the trauma still carried by my ancestors. They're meant to help us understand the origins of the pain and what needs to be transmuted so that we can shift that energy in this lifetime. Traumatic energies are often passed down from generation to generation, and it's important to work through them.

My husband, children, and I have all done some trauma work, but many members of my family have yet to make the effort. They're still asleep to it. They don't realize they're operating on autopilot, unknowingly carrying the energies and patterns of their ancestors, like my great-grandmother, who remains lost and confused earthside.

I'm scheduled for a session again soon, but this practice is passive. It teaches you to trust your intuition and drum as you observe what is happening inside you. Interestingly, this process mirrors what we do in brainspotting; we identify the brainspot and then observe what happens internally. After that session, I definitely felt some relief. There is still anger, and I still have work to do, but the wisdom I've gained from her gifts has been invaluable. It's also kind of nice to have a process where I'm not the one doing all the heavy lifting.

In the end, I lay down for a bit, and we did a soul retrieval. Afterward, I take in the updated version of myself that we've worked to uncover.

Typically, after these sessions, I receive a lot of wisdom and insights, which I'll refer to as "downloads." These downloads bring new knowledge, and I carry them with me until the next experience. It's a continual process of growth. There are many terms for what we've done that I'm not familiar with, but I'm still learning. I'm actively working with my experiences, and I'm even taking an online class that she created.

You could say I'm in the thick of it right now! Working with her and Tito is helping me immensely, a combination of practices to support the healing energies for my ancestors. My confidence is growing, and my ability to channel is strengthening. I'm hearing things more clearly and trusting myself more, even though I still have a skeptical side that does try to get in the way.

Roots of my Skeptical Side

Speaking of which…my skepticism begins with my family. After the abuse from my uncle, nobody believed me. My grandmother, in particular, was skeptical.

When she tried to gaslight me into believing nothing had happened with my uncle, I embarrassed her in the grocery store.

Everyone believed my uncle. It is very sad, really. My memories came back when I was 13 years old. I had dissociated them, and I am not even sure when the sexual abuse began. I know it was under the age of 8. It was during a time when my parents were separated, and they needed someone to watch my sister and me. No one wanted to believe he was capable of such a thing.

Except, thank goodness, my parents. They believed me when I shared what happened. My dad confronted my uncle and tried to make him go to counseling. I heard he went once and never went back. If that *is* true, several counselors let our family down.

No one reported what happened to me to the police.

I told my school counselor, my parents told a marriage counselor, and my uncle went to a counselor. All were mandatory reporters, and no one reported it. Unfortunately, nothing came of it. He went once, never returned, and no one followed up. We all just pretended it didn't happen. I ended up not seeing my grandparents, my other uncle, or cousins after that.

My grandmother passed away during COVID. Her death was far from peaceful. I met with a medium and he immediately told me my grandmother was coming through, apologizing, "I'm so, so sorry, please forgive me." Since then, things have eased for me. While I still don't understand how the women in the family could jeopardize the children, my anger toward the women in my ancestry has diminished significantly.

But I still harbor a fair amount of healthy skepticism.

Human Design

Another lens that's been of great help to my healing is the framework of Human Design. Human Design is a holistic self-discovery system that blends ancient wisdom with modern science to offer a unique blueprint of your energetic makeup. It combines elements of astrology, the *I Ching*, *Kabbalah*, the Chakra system, and quantum physics to reveal how you are uniquely wired to make decisions, interact with others, and navigate life.

At its core, Human Design helps you understand your natural strengths, tendencies, and life purpose by generating a personalized body graph based on your birth time, date, and place. Rather than prescribing a fixed path, it encourages living in alignment with your authentic self, honoring your intuition, and deconditioning from societal expectations. It's a powerful tool for personal growth, relationships, and embodying your fullest potential with clarity and confidence.

I had a friend recommend that I get my Human Design reading, as I was searching for a mentor at the time. I was seeking guidance and validation for my journey. My Human Design is a 6-2, which corresponds to the role model or Buddha archetype.

Although the location and birthdate requirements may suggest astrology, Human Design is far more complex. It integrates various philosophies based on your birth details, offering a deep and personalized reading. I like to think of it as a "Soul Reading."

While Human Design is often compared to systems like the Enneagram, it's much more intricate. Imagine the Myers-Briggs test, but on steroids and combined with other personality assessments, and then you've reached the complexity of Human Design.

I have two people I turn to for Human Design readings. One of them is a gentleman based in Colorado Springs who wears a crystal crown on his head. I wasn't expecting that when I first met him, but I could immediately tell he was very intuitive and spiritual. Since I was searching for guidance, I decided to get a soul reading from him. The reading focused on my journey here on Earth, and it was incredibly accurate, confirming that I'm a natural role model and leader.

Though I've gone through trauma, I also have an innate connection to the divine, and I often receive "downloads," as I've mentioned. I don't always trust these insights at first, but I absorb the wisdom they carry. The world of Human Design can get a bit complex, with all the various philosophies melded together, but at its core, it helps you understand why you're here on Earth.

The reading was nothing short of amazing. It gave me a boost of confidence and insight into my business, even predicting that I'd blossom at a certain age. That prediction came true, and it was truly incredible to hear about my experiences from such a spiritual perspective.

Because of my Human Design, many things come naturally to me, and that doesn't always sit well with others.

The second person I go to for readings, a woman who read my Human Design, told me that many people want what I have. That's where the role model aspect comes in. She warned me that people would often copy me, and she was right. I've experienced it more times than I can count.

When it happens without acknowledgment or credit, I remind myself that being a role model means others will mirror what I do. That perspective helps me stay grounded and keeps me from getting too upset. Given who I am and how I show up, it makes sense that this would happen. It doesn't mean I don't have boundaries; it just means I can meet them with more grace.

I get frustrated at times, thinking, "I don't want to be a leader. I don't want to manage people." It often feels like, no matter where I go, I end up being a leader. It just seems to happen organically; I'll share my thoughts, and suddenly, everyone's listening. The woman who gave me my reading talked about how magnetic I am and how people are drawn to my energy. I hear this often from others, too; they say I'm real and easy to talk to. I am mindful of always wanting to be humble. It is also ok to be confident. Recognizing our gifts in our lifetime can support our personal evolution.

I also learned that I'm here to study. Human Design is a tool that helps me understand my soul's path, showing me what I need to learn. Even before hearing this reading, I had decided to stop the cycle of generational trauma.

From a young age, I was willing to speak out. I've always been a truth-teller, which gets me into trouble at times, but it's not a bad thing to do. I get divine downloads, and this woman understood all of that because it was all written in my soul reading.

This comes up often with the people I mentor, and I usually recommend getting a Human Design reading. Not a single person has come back without saying it was absolutely amazing. It helps people gain clarity on their purpose and why they're here, and it also allows me to talk about my own gifts.

Human Design is a powerful tool that helps you understand where you are on your path. One of the things I've learned through my reading is that I will benefit from listening to more music. It's one of my gateways of energy, through which energy comes into me and how I reflect it back to the world.

My husband and I did a reading together once, and it was interesting to see how some of our conflicts stem from our different Human Designs. He's someone who actively goes after things, while I'm more of a generator, meaning I'm supposed to wait for things to come to me. This can be difficult for me, especially because I tend to initiate, which can sometimes leave people upset. People in my life often call me the "golden child" because they notice that things come easily to me. The truth is, I take the time to think things through before deciding whether or not to take an opportunity. These are just some of the characteristics of my Human Design.

As a "Buddha" in this system, my purpose is to have experiences and share them with people so they can learn too. That's what I'm doing here. I'm a role model, and I give others the information they need to heal. Human Design has been such a validating tool, a real eye-opener, reminding me that I'm exactly where I'm supposed to be. There are times when I feel mentally lost, but this reading reassured me that I'm doing exactly what I was meant to do.

Intuition

You might call it a hunch, or listening to your gut, but fundamentally, intuition is a thought or sensation that comes to you and then flows out into the world. I often believe it's something divine. There are times when wisdom comes out of my mouth, and I think, "Where did that come from?"

People will ask me to repeat myself, but I can't. I have no idea where it comes from sometimes.

It's also a physical sensation, like when I healed my ancestors. I got full-body goosebumps that started at my knees and traveled up through my chest and arms. When I feel that, it's like Spirit saying, "Right on." It's a kind of validation.

Another way I know intuition is at work is when I receive a visual or a thought, and then a synchronous moment unfolds. Last October, I had a conversation with my coach and asked if she was open to intuition. She agreed, and I shared some of my intuitive hits with her. I heard the words "Lost Sister," and she was taken aback. She told me that just the night before, she had been talking to her partner about how lost she felt about her sister. That's what I mean by synchronicity. She then shared her whole story, and to this day, I still get goosebumps thinking about how spot-on it was.

Since I was a kid, I could always see patterns in people, but I didn't realize that was intuition. I assumed everyone could do that. Turns out, not everyone can. As we talked about, I'm a truthteller, and part of the challenge I faced as a child was speaking the truth. Not everyone is ready to hear the truth, and that often came back to bite me. I was a curious kid, and I remember asking my mom when I was about 5 or 6 years old, "Why is everyone asleep?"

She was confused by that, so I explained that people often say one thing but do another. I was talking about alignment and consciousness, and did not know that at the time. She got annoyed, which wasn't my intention. At the time, I didn't know if people were just lying when they spoke. What I realized later is that people weren't lying; they were simply unconscious, operating on autopilot. This is where the intersection of spirituality and intuition comes in, working hand-in-hand.

Thinking back to that day on the beach with David, I'll never forget when he asked me to be a trainer. At that moment, I felt like my life had changed forever, and I could feel it in my body. It was a huge validation for my younger self. As a kid, I always knew I was meant for something big, but I had given up by my 20s. I thought my shot had passed; that is, until I took a massive risk and went to New York for brainspotting.

I was taking David out to lunch, and as we got there, I started to open up. He saw my creativity, something I hadn't recognized in myself. Up until then, I thought I wasn't that smart. Back in elementary school, I knew my brain didn't work quite right, but I didn't know why. This confusion tormented me for years. It wasn't until I was in grad school, studying trauma, that I understood my brain didn't work "right" because of trauma.

After doing EMDR and brainspotting, I took some IQ tests, and my score went up almost 20 points! Turns out, my trauma had been holding me back, along with undiagnosed ADHD. When I was growing up, they didn't always look for neurodivergence in girls. People assumed only boys had ADHD, but I definitely showed the symptoms. Always interrupting, very social, and dysregulated, though I didn't have the fancy words for that back then. It wasn't until grad school that I understood.

David was the first person to see my "problems" as creative power. My scattered focus was a gift in his eyes, which was shocking to me. I never imagined my struggles could be anything but faults, let alone something I could be gifted with. I started noticing that people were saying things like, "Hey, you know, you can work on both Windows and Mac." These are above-average technical skills I have, which I didn't fully appreciate. My husband was a tech teacher, so he could operate on all the systems. But not everyone picks up on things as easily as I do, and I was just starting to realize that.

After David saw me and I became a trainer, my clients began healing like crazy. I started receiving emails from people telling me I've saved their lives. Only recently did I realize I've been channeling during my sessions. Spirit's completely inside of me, guiding my intuition. I take risks and get deeply attuned to my clients, listening on a higher level. Like their soul begins speaking to me in a different language than the words coming out of their mouths. My clients lead the way, and my intuition supports the attuned relationship we have.

For example, a gentleman I worked with just this week told me his wife only sees the bad in him, and nothing he does is good enough. What I really heard, though, was, "I just want to be loved. I want to be told I'm a good boy." That's what I hear beneath the surface of what he's saying. I listen to the younger, developmentally arrested parts of them, and when we do healing together, I hold space and at times speak to those parts.

I had a similar experience with a woman who saw two parts of herself, one of which wouldn't speak to or listen to her. I told her to whisper, "I've got you. I see you, and I've got you," to that part. It worked! That's precisely what that part needed, and she burst into tears. This experience unlocked something in her system.

Another example of this happened when my husband and I went to Lake Geneva for our anniversary. We decided to get a couple's massage, and as we passed by a cemetery, I saw a man in a gray jacket and pants with a little beanie on top of his head. I kept seeing him in my mind, and I eventually asked him to leave, as this was in the middle of a massage with my husband. He wouldn't go.

He kept repeating to me, "Tell her about the little girl." Over and over again. I didn't know what this meant, so I asked what he was trying to say, but I didn't get an answer. He just kept insisting, "Tell her." Once we finished our massage and got dressed, I told my husband what had happened. We went to the lobby, and when I opened the door, a woman was sitting at the desk. I decided to meet my husband upstairs and went over to speak with her.

I asked her if she was open to intuitive hits. She assumed I must be a psychic medium, but I told her I have strong intuition. I then said, "Someone is telling me I need to tell you about this little girl." I explained that she looked like she had passed away and was with the man I had seen.

The woman began to cry and told me that she had lost a little boy, but there was someone on the staff who had lost a little girl. I told her, "I was told to tell you that she's okay and that he's with her." That was all the information I had, but she was deeply grateful. It felt a bit uncomfortable for me, but it's always worth it when I take a risk, and it brings comfort to others.

It took me a long time to get comfortable with opening up. When I was a little girl, I would see spirits, and I was made fun of for it. Kids can be cruel. This went on for years, especially in elementary school. I think back to my friend Kim, who passed away. Her mom grew increasingly annoyed with me each time I came over. Kim's grandmother had died in the house, and on nights when I stayed over, she would show up at three o'clock in the morning, trying to talk to me.

What happened was I'd see the spirit and wake Kim up. Then, we'd have to wake her mom, and then I'd need to call my dad to come pick me up. This went on for years, and between the teasing at school and upsetting my friend's mom, I eventually learned to shut it down.

There's so much suffering in this world. If I can help people believe in life after death and offer some hope, then maybe I can find the courage to share that with others. As I've become more comfortable sharing my gifts, I've seen the real impact they have on people. That's what makes this book so special. If you relate to my experiences, know you're not alone. I see you.

Mediumship and Psychics

When I hold space for demonstrations at the brainspotting trainings or with clients, I can read people pretty easily. I rely on my intuition to connect with and hear parts of their soul that many others can't. I do not make assumptions about people. I listen inside and hear the whispers of intuition.

There are different terms for the types of energies people can read, and they aren't all the same. For example, a psychic focuses on reading a person or their personality, while a medium connects with spirits—those who have passed on and come through. Not every psychic is a medium, but every medium is psychic.

As I've had more psychic experiences as an adult, I've had to set boundaries. No more nighttime stuff, I don't need to be spooked in the parking lot! I'm happy to listen during the day, though. If you remember, after Kim passed, she told me, "You need to be a death doula." I looked it up, and I told her I didn't want to participate. I didn't want to be surrounded by spirits, leaving or witnessing things like that.

Shortly after this, I had a client who was a death doula, and I had to hold space for the work she did. Not long after, I started seeing TikToks from a woman who's a nurse. She had permission to show the different stages of death and spoke about families seeing their loved ones' souls transition. When these videos started popping up on my feed, I thought to myself, "Damn it, Kim, I know this is you doing this." Who says spirits can't use the algorithm?

I continued holding space for the mediums and psychics who came to me, placing my focus on them while doubting my own gifts. I had a few colleagues who came to me during one of my first brainspotting trainings. They were Indigenous and actually worked with spirits themselves. They knew I was gifted, and years later, we all giggled about it because I used to be so afraid of accepting it and tapping into the world of spirituality.

Pink Bunny Story

I once had an experience with a client whose son had been murdered. Throughout the session, I kept hearing "pink bunny, pink bunny, pink bunny", over and over again. In my mind, I wanted it to stop. I was wondering what the obsession with a pink bunny was. I was sort of beating myself up for these repetitive thoughts until I finally just asked her at the end of the session if "pink bunny" meant anything, and her jaw dropped.

She told me her son had a pink bunny piggy bank and asked me how I knew. I told her it was my intuition, but she had assumed I must be a psychic.

If you're a clinician or healer reading this and aren't ready to fully embrace the role of a psychic medium, I understand. I highly recommend exploring Clinical Intuition. When working within the dual attunement frame of brainspotting, we can synchronize with our clients and exchange energy within this biofield. This biofield contains collective information, and when we remain present and open to what emerges, we can gain beautiful insights that are deeply beneficial for the client.

These experiences might feel strange or difficult to explain, but they are what make clinical intuition what it is. It is okay if you're uncomfortable with the subject. It happens to all of us, and there is no singular way of doing this kind of work. There is collective information in the biofield. Honestly, I think we are all capable of being psychics, intuitive, and healers; it's only a matter of how open we are to these possibilities.

Our brains and bodies are amazing beyond all measure, and we're capable of more than what we give ourselves credit for. We limit and diminish ourselves based on societal norms and what we've been conditioned to believe. We all have these gifts, and through practices like brainspotting, we can work to enhance them.

I really think brainspotting enhances this stuff; that's actually what led Heather Corbet and me to create the "Brainspotting, Spirituality and Intuition" class, the idea of the "Soul Flow" group/community membership, with the tagline, *Putting the Science in the Woo.*

It turns out that lots of people want to explore their soul and spirituality, which they can do through their faith or belief in certain traditions. Lisa Miller's book, *The Awakened Brain,* presents research showing the connection between mental health and spirituality. A couple of studies in the book found that the following individuals were less likely to develop depression: 80% of children who shared a spiritual life with their mothers, as well as 35-75% of teenagers with an intense personal spirituality. This included when faced with risk factors such as parental depression, poverty, or chronic stress. This suggests that a spiritual foundation within the family can be an important mental health strategy (Miller, 2022).

An important distinction should be noted that the spirituality in the above-mentioned studies didn't exclusively include religion, or the attendance of a weekly service, but did reference a deep inner connection to something greater than themselves. That inner connection builds a buffer against life's challenges, allowing the teen to show greater resilience through emotional and social challenges. These findings question the current belief of keeping mental health separate from spiritual development in youth-focused prevention. These studies aren't merely anecdotal either. MRI scans show that on a neurological level, individuals with high spiritual engagement have increased cortical thickness in the parts of the brain typically thinned by depression. This difference in structure indicates that spirituality can shape and fortify the brain.

Miller explains that about 30% of our spiritual orientation is inherited through genetics, while the other 70% is shaped by our environment, experiences, and practice. This idea supports that while some people may have a natural predisposition toward spiritual awareness, anyone can learn through effort and support. Spiritual capacity is not fixed, and nurturing it through meditation or other means can strengthen emotional resilience. It isn't just an emotional or philosophical construct. Miller's work reframes spirituality as an essential aspect of health. By integrating spirituality into mental health, educators, parents, and clinicians can tap into a new healing pathway.

In our rebranded "Spirit Code" membership group, we explore the beliefs that shape our achievements, ways to invite more flow into our lives, and how to truly live at our fullest potential. We share practices for manifesting your dream life and feeling fully alive. The old name "Soul Flow" reflects our focus on intentionally guiding the soul into a state of flow, so we can allow our best, most aligned life to naturally unfold.

Our training continues to evolve as well. We're also introducing immersion experiences, where we'll teach these practices in a deeper, more experiential way, supporting more people in connecting with their spirituality, intuition, and ability to manifest. We're blending what we've learned through our own lived experiences with what science is now beginning to validate and understand.

Channeling

Channeling is the process of connecting with Spirit and receiving, or downloading, information both physically and non-physically. This can happen through talk therapy, brainspotting, writing, music, art, and other forms of expression. It's about taking in information on a deeper level.

For me, channeling is about helping people heal and holding space with them before and after a brainspotting session. Spirit speaks through me to convey different messages to the soul before me. I translate what the mind is saying in a way that people can understand. I have been told I am a bridge between the worlds. I work on sharing information so that others can receive it without fear or hesitation. I attuned to them, and I can share the information in a way that allows folks to hear it.

When I sit across from someone who is deeply wounded, defensive, or collapsed, something divine guides me on how to hold the space as though something is reaching into their soul and shifting their energy. This is the genius of their own subcortical brain. I believe our souls, limbic systems align so that their soul opens to new possibilities, to the potential change they desire.

There are times when I'll think, "Where the hell did that come from?" after saying something truly profound. I could never have come up with it on my own. People occasionally come back to me with things they've written down from our session, telling me how beautiful it was. Sometimes, I can hardly remember what I said. I truly believe the divine is present in these moments. I am a mere conduit.

To begin, I call in my guides (those white, flowy beings) to arrive, and at times, I can see and feel them. I often receive visuals, although sometimes they're a bit unconventional. For example, I've seen hands being held above my client's shoulders from behind, and I see energy and light about their shoulders. This is energy work known as Reiki. I have also seen hands at the top of people's heads with energy going in.

I experience a very physical sense of knowing, validating my experience. I get full-body goosebumps. I never understood why until I started making connections again as an adult. Whenever something truly important comes out of my mouth, I get goosebumps, and that's my validation of a deeper channeling. It feels like someone is helping me, and what comes out isn't of my making.

This coming weekend, I'm hosting what I call a "Deep Dive" session. I love these sessions, where therapists and healers come together for the better part of a day to intentionally work on something. It's a straightforward process designed to release and shift the energy of whatever is bothering them. Or to expand into a desire they want to manifest in their life. If people are open, we tap into their intentions, but I always ask for permission first. I've worked with many spiritual individuals and shamans, and one of my pet peeves is when they are dismissive about consent.

Sometimes, I sense information, but not everyone is ready to receive it, so I always make sure to check with the person first. Some people have told me, "No, I really don't want to know," and that's perfectly fine with me. On the other hand, when people are open to hearing it, I make sure to share the information as politely and lovingly as possible. It's not always something they want to hear, so it's important to remain open to that possibility.

Channeling with a Client

If you want to share a channeling experience, it must come from love and not ego. The difference between the two is personal, and you may need to figure out what that means for you. For me, I can usually tell the difference in my intentions quite easily. If I want to share something because I think the information is so amazing and that people will love me for it, that comes straight from the ego. However, when I sit, feel grounded, and the information flows repeatedly, it is usually coming from a place of love and the divine. I stay mindful and observe the other person while they speak.

One thing that's very important is asking for permission before sharing information with anyone. If I sense something in the space between us, I may ask if they are open to receiving feedback. I make it clear that they can take or leave whatever resonates with them, and people typically respond well to that soft approach.

Another method I use is offering an intuitive insight. I want to be very clear here that it is outside of doing brainspotting with them. This usually happens after a session, before, or when casually speaking about something important to them.

Some vulnerable people may take what I say as fact, so I always remind them that they do not need to take everything I say to heart. I lead by telling all of my clients that they can "take what they like and leave the rest." Ultimately, they get to decide what feels true, not me. Free will and choice must always be involved, and I never want anyone to feel obligated to act in a certain way.

I need to be aware of the impact I have as much as possible, so I can avoid triggering a shame response. I'm hyper-conscious of how I communicate so my words don't unintentionally cause harm. All that is shared must come from a loving space. Even with the best intentions, I can still make mistakes, and that's part of being human. I stay open to repairing any missteps. If someone comes back and says I've messed up, I need to be ready to have an open and honest conversation about that.

What often happens is that people come in with high expectations, seeking detailed proof, but that's not what Spirit typically provides. Spirit frequently communicates through images, symbols, and stories, clever ways to bypass our defenses and deliver messages. Spirit will find a way to work around your defense system to get information to you. Over time, Spirit works with your inner dictionary to deliver their messages. It is up to you to study and practice to gain an understanding.

For example, I was recently in an intensive with a practitioner whose spouse had died by suicide during their divorce process. Not knowing this beforehand, one evening, as we're talking, the topic of her previous marriage came up. She mentioned that she had been married before, but her husband had completed suicide. I expressed my condolences, telling her how sorry I was that she had to go through such a difficult experience.

As soon as she had said that, though, I felt him next to me. I felt uncomfortable, but I said the woman's name and asked if she was open to hearing some information. She agreed, and I explained that I had no intention of doing this, but that I was getting messages from him that he wanted me to share with her. What is interesting is that she then told me he had actually tried to do this with another medium the past year, but she said no at the time. She wasn't ready. She said yes this time, and she was able to listen to what he had to say.

She met this guy in recovery, got married to him, and he continued to relapse. There was an overall very chaotic energy about him in life, and she filed for divorce and then moved out. He kept a journal and wrote down his plans to end his life. He wrote about how he was going to do it and detailed the process. I don't remember his age, but he planned it for his birthday.

Luckily, the woman listened to her intuition because on the day of his Birthday, she did not go home and was with her current partner. Her intuition told her not to be in the house. He killed himself in the car, parked in the driveway of her home, but she was gone.

Through our discussion, we found out that she still has all the letters and information from his death. We discussed why she was holding onto that energy in her home, and she wasn't sure why. I told her I could hear him saying that it was okay for her to let go and that he was essentially asking for her forgiveness. She assured me she wasn't holding a grudge, and I explained that the energy in her home was the last piece she needed to release.

Interestingly, two months prior, I had hosted a training session at her home. I knew even less about her at the time, but I heard her mom's voice speaking to me. I told her that her mom was singing the song, "I want you to know how precious you are."

The woman immediately started to tear up and told me that I was staying in the room with all her mom's things. After the reading, when her ex appeared, she mentioned that her ex's belongings were also in that room with her mom's things. She was planning on releasing the items into the local river. "It sounds important that you do that," I told her, and assured her he was okay with this release.

After he said his piece, I told him, "It's time for you to go now." He didn't want to go at first, but he had fulfilled his purpose in helping her. I think he wanted to stick around to ensure she got rid of everything, but I reminded him that she had free will. There was a clear shift in the energy after he left.

About an hour later, she came into the room and asked if he was gone. I replied, "Yes, he's gone," and shared with her the little battle he had experienced. I told her that he had to go now, as he needed to do deeper human work. I explained what had happened afterward, and then I left. It felt like it never happened at all.

This is what I'm talking about, though, how Spirit can be sneaky. I'm currently mentoring with a psychic medium, and when he puts me on the spot, I experience performance anxiety. I'm still struggling with the skepticism that exists within me. I can be having a casual conversation, and just like in this last example, spirits can show up unexpectedly. I'm not always prepared for it, but there are wise spirits that will always find a way to come through. Just listen.

—————

Costa Rica

Nature is everything to me, a natural holder for the nervous system, carrying the rhythm of life in every sound: cicadas buzzing, birds calling, monkeys chattering, and the countless other voices of the wild. This is my perspective—my mentors, like Tito, might describe it differently, but I left Costa Rica with a deepened appreciation for the living world.

The brothers shared with us many ways to create an altar for our *Khipus*. They encouraged offerings drawn from the elements, bringing flowers, a bottle of wine, or other gifts that honor the earth, spirits, and our ancestors. The Peruvian healers hold ceremonies that open a doorway to connection with these elements. We first met them in Peru, then gathered again at Teri's in Costa Rica to continue our education.

Music was everywhere, bird whistles, rattles, drumming, flutes, all woven together with chanting voices in the background until the sound seemed to absorb you. These practices are designed to shift energy and consciousness. I remember during our personal work, each of us received a whistle to support our self-practice. I went into nature, found my place, and used the whistle to call in the elements for my intention, to shift into love. It was a practice I did alone, surrounded by the living world. And now, wherever I am, these are the practices I return to.

Another process I've brought home with me is working with scented waters. I have Florida Water and something called *Derosa*, which is rose petal-infused. I love the smell, and it's applied directly to the palms, then enters the olfactory system. It's said you're to rub your hands together, seven times, and then clap to activate the energy in the scented waters to activate its clearing properties. We smell and take in the scents, and it works as an easy way to shift some energy if something feels sticky and icky.

These feelings are unavoidable at times, and another personal practice I do is saying a prayer to incorporate with my Peruvian practices. A psychic I worked with told me that if I wanted to clear my energy, I needed something short and sweet that was meaningful to me. He suggested a prayer that goes, "Jesus, son of Joseph, Jesus son of Mary, Jesus son of God, Jesus son of Man ground the Divine in my body." I then touch my third eye and my heart while rubbing my hands together with the Florida Water seven times, and then clap loudly four times to activate the oils in the water. This helps clear energy.

Another practice I learned from Tito is utilizing different hand positions. In yoga practice, you might call these *mudras*. In Tito's tradition, for example, placing your thumbs together or putting your hand on your chest is one of the ways for you to be connected to your *Munay*. It is almost as if we're hugging ourselves, but we're feeling the *Munay* within us, our love. Through some of these practices, we are chanting. Others are more physical, but here I'm just introducing a few snippets of the processes that are out there. We can't expect to cover everything, and I've barely begun to scratch the surface.

A New Kind of Knowing

At the end of the day, however you look at it, we are learning to shift energy through new practices, moving our bodies, or bringing in music. We just have to tap into different processes to activate the energy we need to send our love out, or to release whatever is holding us back. These are ancient traditions that have been around for thousands of years, and Western culture is beginning to finally acknowledge their wisdom.

Additionally, there is a growing amount of modern research out there to back these traditions. An organization called Collective Healing Initiative (CHI), led by Dr. Shamini Jain, a university professor who worked with Richard Davidson at UW-Madison, also incorporates practices like mantra and chanting. Dr. Jain discusses the biofield and how she and a bunch of other researchers are researching to show that practices like Reiki are real (Jain 2025).

They're also researching to prove sound shifts energy. They are researching frequency and how important music is in healing. They are starting to use science to prove how all of these things shift the central nervous system. It makes sense, we're electrical beings.

There are different ways this is already showing itself; we know they're using vibration for medical purposes these days. The "Safe and Sound" and "Rest and Restore" protocols, based on Polyvagal theory, are yet another example. A healing system that utilizes the inner ear and music frequencies to shift our autonomic nervous system patterns.

Another example, if you have a kidney stone, there are some places in the world where you can go to sit in a tank, where they actually vibrate your body to break the kidney stone apart. Think about it, they are also using lasers for different treatments. Red light therapy has a lot of research on how it affects your body, increases your immune system, and even helps your brain. There are all kinds of alternative options that the Western world was never open to, that we're just opening up to now, and it is absolutely wonderful.

In a painfully simplified nutshell, we're learning that our brains and bodies are powerful self-healers when they are connected. People are beginning to reject pharmaceuticals, but it can be scary to take a stand against a multi-million dollar industry. Regardless, more and more people are taking back their own health. It feels like there's a big crash ahead in our medical field. A shift is happening.

If you're a therapist who's still more cognitive or Western in your framework, please hear me when I say, I too fought this tooth and nail. In turn, I've legitimized myself through education my entire life. I am not saying that education isn't valuable, but experiential learning and being in the presence of another culture open you up in a different way. Going to a different country, with different cultural norms and beliefs, for example, will push your comfort zone differently than being in your inherited Western culture.

By seeking experiences that are out of the ordinary, when I hold space for another person, I can be confident that I can hold space for whatever comes my way. Just the other day, I had a friend of mine reach out to me about a practitioner who led a ketamine workshop. They had done a lot of their own personal work, but were looking for somebody who could hold a unique space wherever they were going to go. My friend told me I immediately came to mind for people who can help because I would go with the flow, and I rarely get freaked out by unusual things, preferring to approach new ideas with curiosity. And there's that word, flow, again…

Recently, I received an email from a practitioner needing reassurance about a spiritual experience with a client. She thought something was wrong and couldn't help but freak out about it. She shared what happened, and it honestly sounded beautiful to me, which is what I told her.

I made sure she knew I was curious and assured her that it sounded like an amazing, beautiful experience that she should honor. Just by sending that email, she calmed down. She thanked me for giving her reassurance. When we have no context for what we observe as healers, our negativity bias in our brain can take over. In brainspotting, we learn to replace fear with love and curiosity.

This is something so many of us need. We tend to hide our feelings, and my goal here is to offer support and to let us all be curious. We need safe communities where people can share these things, explore, and not get bullied, ridiculed, or made to feel less than.

Impact of Real Experience

As mentioned, an image of my great-grandmother once came to me. She was stepping into a boat, heading toward a place of wisdom. This is the kind of stuff you can't apply science to, but I know the relief I felt in my central system, and vividly visualized this experience. You can't exactly conduct a research study on that, but, well, I know it happened. This was a pivotal moment for me, especially as a skeptic myself. It was all so spontaneous. It felt like a divine process. Everything happens for a reason, and I'm simply listening to my intuition. I experienced a release in my body after this experience. This is what we call shifts. A gentle letting go of something that had been imprinted in my central nervous system.

For my healing, I needed to clear out the anger and rage from my ancestors who weren't awake. They were traumatized people, and I'm looking to find my way toward forgiveness (or at least understanding). I don't know exactly how to get there, but I know I want to release this anger from my body. It's a process I'm still figuring out, but the important thing is that none of us are on this journey alone, truly!

My experience brought me tremendous relief, and it deepened my understanding of Peruvian and Celtic practices. The book *Attuned* talks about ancestral healing (Hübl, 2023). explores epigenetics and how our ancestors' experiences live within us, literally within our bodies. Another book, *Ancestral Medicine*, helps you learn to get in contact with your lineage and spirits to support generational trauma healing (Foor, 2017). I am learning to combine brainspotting with ancestral medicine to further deepen my work with clearing out generational trauma from my body.

There's no science yet on how we heal epigenetic energy that we carry in our bodies.

Consider the extensive amount of research conducted on the Holocaust. We know through the thorough research we have on Holocaust survivors that PTSD symptomology echoes through generations, for children who did not experience the Holocaust firsthand. PTSD symptoms still get passed down; it's a generational transmission.

The books that are coming out now talk about the need to also heal the generations that are inside of our bodies. Indigenous people already know this. They say we can heal seven years forward and seven years back.

Einstein has said, "And certainly we should take care not to make the intellect our god; it has, of course, powerful muscles, but no personality. It cannot lead, it can only serve; and it is not fastidious in its choices of a leader" (Einstein, 1950).

Western culture has become overly focused on research and "proof." However, there have always been other ways of knowing, and even the most knowledgeable individuals acknowledge that! More and more wisdom is emerging, and it's not based on science; it's based on lived experience. That's why I love this book title, *Sacred Knowing*. I see that we are learning to trust and explore different ways of knowing.

We've talked a little bit about the magnetic and energetic being that you are, and I'm sure there are a lot of healers who will read this and go figure out what their Human Design number is. It builds confidence, makes everything make sense, and can validate your path. It also helps you recognize your gifts. I've been told everything I do turns to gold, and quite often it does. That will piss off a lot of the people in my life, but I've had the patience to wait. I do the hard work of going inside and work on intentional daily life practices so that I can manifest what is in my heart. This phenomenon also shows up in my Human Design reading. I am here to be a role model.

People ask me why I'm doing so much. Between studying Celtic and Peruvian practices and being a brainspotting trainer, they wonder why I have all these different focuses. Honestly, I'm just following my intuition and opening myself up to different possibilities. I'm being led.

I've also been told that I need to learn more, especially because I'm feeling confused and overwhelmed by Celtic practices. Even some of the Peruvian practices are a struggle for me at times. However, after that experience with my ancestors, I began to understand a little more. You can't just learn all of this through science.

I must sit with something and wait for it to come to me, then make a decision. My Human Design shows me this is exactly the way it needs to be for me to make decisions. My Human Design says that opportunities will come to me, and my job is to wait until I feel neutral about making the decision. This is where clarity comes from. I also look to see if this opportunity is aligned with goals I've set for myself. When it is not, this guides me to say no more often.

Anything that happens in my life is usually because I had a divine download, I listened to my intuition, and then made it happen once I knew it was aligned with what I wanted to bring into my life. When my husband and I were getting couples' massages, and I told the gentleman to leave my head, I learned then and there that I can, indeed, set boundaries with spirits.

I didn't know this at the time, but I'm not alone here. A lot of psychics will tell you that you can set boundaries with spirits. I just thought they came and went, and I just had to deal with it. I was also a little skeptical if I was making stuff up, but that is what was happening as I remember it.

Now I know I am able to stand up for myself, and that's when I started to be able to tell them not to come during the dark. It traumatizes me when the spirits come at night, but allowing them in the day makes things according to *my* boundaries. That has helped me feel like I have a little bit more power and choice, which makes me more comfortable with it. I can use this gift in the ways I am comfortable. Brainspotting opened the door to these gifts. Having spirits appear, or I will hear spirits during healing work or teaching, has made it safer for me to believe. It's like they are helping me accept my gifts through brainspotting.

On many different planes, it's unnerving to have someone in your space in the evening. Now all I have to say is, "Hey, we haven't agreed to this, you have to leave." Or "back up." Then, I feel the spirit leaving immediately. I am continuing to work on this through brainspotting so that I can free my energy up and be more open and unfearful. While I am still triggered at times, working through these real experiences gives me much more control over my body.

CHAPTER 6

Manifesting

What is Manifestation?

When people first hear about manifestation, they often think of it as a big secret. Some become obsessed with trying to make things happen, referring to it as "energy," while others dismiss it as mere "woo-woo."

According to *Mind Magic* by James Doty, manifestation is easily and often misunderstood. He defines it as "the process of bringing desires, goals, and intentions into reality by aligning thoughts, emotions, and actions with a clear vision" (Doty, 2024). It blends mindset, energy, and focused effort.

True manifestation isn't mere wishful thinking, but a dynamic interplay of belief, intuition, and conscious action that shapes our outcomes. At its core, manifestation is about grit and perseverance. When entering a flow state, the brain begins to make new connections, electrically linking neurons that help recognize opportunities. This happens because the brain has understood, "This is my intention." In response, the brain begins to focus on making it a reality.

What is "Flow State"?

Several great researchers have explored the concept of flow, one of my favorites being Mihaly Csikszentmihalyi, a Hungarian-American psychologist, who defines flow as a "state of complete immersion in an activity that experiences deep focus, enjoyment, and effortless involvement" (Csikszentmihalyi, 1990). I also took a class with Steven Kotler, who builds on Csikszentmihalyi's work, describing flow as a peak experience (Kotler, 2019).

Flow is a state of deep absorption where time appears to stand still. Personally, when in a state of flow, I lose track of time; I can forget to eat and drink, I'm so completely immersed in the creative process. It feels automatic, everything clicking effortlessly into place. It's thrilling, inspiring, a space where creativity just *flows* out.

Flow helps us reach our creative potential through peak experiences, such as being in the zone or experiencing deep gratitude. I've absolutely reached this point before. Psychologist Abraham Maslow asserts that peak experiences play a crucial role in self-actualization (Maslow, 1954).

To be "in the zone" is to feel fully present, alive, and utterly absorbed in what you're doing. The moments when time seems to melt away and you're running purely on intuition and inspiration. However, being in the zone, combined with the feeling of awe—a concept Dacher Keltner explores in his book AWE (Keltner, 2023)—can create an utterly profound transformational experience.

Awe is that sense of wonder and vastness that takes you out of yourself, reminding us that life holds more magic and meaning than we can put into words. It's the feeling when something special, such as nature, a work of art, or a moment of connection, takes your breath away and leaves you changed.

I felt this deeply the first time I stood on a cliff overlooking Machu Picchu. Completely in the zone, soaking in every detail, perfectly present. More than just focus. Awe in its truest sense. The immensity of the ancient city, the mystery carved into every stone, and the realization of the centuries that came before it all struck me at once. I imagined laughter and footsteps echoing from long ago, and in that suspended moment, I felt connected to something timeless and far greater than myself.

Being in the zone of awe isn't just about flow; it's about surrendering to the wonder of being alive, letting gratitude and openness take the lead. These moments not only inspire us, they imprint us, deepening our sense of meaning, belonging, and possibility. When I add a brainspot with this, I can anchor and imprint this new experience into my central nervous system. Practicing doing this daily builds an internal muscle to increase flow, spiritual, intuitive, and awe experiences. Rick Hanson discusses the importance of taking in the good in his book, *Buddha's Brain* (Hanson, 2009).

Peak experiences, flow states, and creativity are all deeply connected. In many ways, they feel like spiritual experiences, as they evoke similar physiological responses. In these moments, we feel lighter, more engaged, and deeply connected.

When I had that peak experience at Machu Picchu, I intentionally felt it in my bones and body. I consciously anchored myself in the moment, imprinting the feeling of that peak experience. This is something we can practice: truly absorbing and internalizing these moments. I remember thinking, "If I can manifest this, what *else* can I manifest?" That question set everything in motion. Soon after, I started organizing travel trips and bringing people to Peru.

I had a similar experience when I was looking to buy a new car. I wanted a red VW Bug. The moment I began seriously searching for one, I started seeing them everywhere. This is how the brain works; once we set an intention, we become attuned to opportunities that were always there, just previously overlooked.

First Manifestation and Intention Memory

As a little girl, I knew I wanted to do something big with my life, and felt confident that I could. However, in my early 20s, that confidence faded, and I felt beaten down. At the time, I didn't fully understand why, but upon reflection, I see I was constantly working on personal growth. I went to therapy, read books on self-improvement and human development, and continued to push forward. I did not realize my traumas were weighing me down, and my system was saturated.

Then came EMDR, my first experience where I physically felt something leave my body. It was a turning point in my life. Looking back, I now see that even before grad school, I was drawn to psychology and human development. I took an unusual number of courses in those areas, and that's when it finally clicked: "Oh, I have PTSD."

In college one winter, on my way to give a speech in one of my classes, I drove down Route 41 in Wisconsin, hitting a patch of black ice. I did a complete 360 on the highway. It was a miracle I didn't get hit by incoming traffic. People veered around me, and then I ended up back in the lane correctly. It was like a shot in a movie. I drove to school, but I couldn't stop shaking, and on top of that, I had to give a presentation for my class.

A fellow student of mine pulled me into a room and gave me headphones with bilateral stimulation music to calm me down. I didn't have much time to even understand what was happening before I could feel stuff leaving my body. I started laughing because I was like, "Oh my God, this is working!" Then, suddenly, I went back to the memory of my abuse at age 7-8. She stopped us, telling me I would need additional work. I didn't know what was going on, but it was the sense of loss of control that connected to the deeper trauma of the abuse.

After that day, I spent two years doing EMDR therapy, and my PTSD symptoms decreased significantly. I was getting better. Finally, I became a therapist myself, working with people who had complex PTSD. Trained in EMDR, I still encountered outlier situations where I couldn't help someone. And of course, those were the cases my brain focused on, frustrated that I couldn't seem to make a difference there.

An intern of mine asked me if I'd heard of brainspotting. I wasn't sure what it was at the time, but she told me that David Grand uses it for performance and trauma. I knew who David Grand was because I was using his bilateral music for clients during EMDR sessions. I decided to take his training. Back in the day, when I took brainspotting in 2009, they did phases one and two together. It was five days straight. My best friend and I went down to Nashville, and we took this training for the first time.

In EMDR, they say, "When you get to a zero, you are finished."

But in brainspotting, "A zero is not a zero."

Brainspotting Theory posits that there's always something deeper within the brain. There are developmental layers in there. Being skeptical, I deliberately worked on something I thought was a zero. For me, this was a memory of my dad coming home and kicking me out of his chair, clicking the remote, and changing the channel while I was watching my show.

My husband clicks the channel often when we are sitting together watching TV. I used to get so triggered and irate, above and beyond what was necessary. This is the memory I worked on. I had worked on this memory with the EMDR, and I realized that I reacted that way to my husband because when my dad did it, I felt like I didn't matter. I didn't feel important, and that's what was triggering me from my husband.

This improved with EMDR, but then, when I processed it with brainspotting, something interesting happened. I was staring at this pointer, and my shoulders started to move uncontrollably. I was like, "What the hell is going on?" My friend was watching me, and I went into a massive network of memories of feeling like I didn't matter and all the fawning behaviors I would do to try to get love and to try to get people to like me. I saw my people-pleasing habits in all my relationships. This was a major coping mechanism for me.

I was like, "Oh my God, it's everywhere in my life!" With people, including my husband, friends, coworkers, and boss. I started to realize that I wasn't being myself, and then all of a sudden, this little eight-year-old popped into my head. That's the age when I was abused.

Eight-year-old me leans forward and says, "Hi…" We started to have a dialogue inside my head. She told me she was me, and I started to cry because she represented a very traumatic point in my life. I worked with her and discussed what had happened with her.

Long story short, at some point, she and I were inside my head and started doing the Macarena. It felt so relieving. I knew I didn't have to do things a certain way anymore. I was in my 40s at this time, and I asked myself, "What do we want to do now?"

I remember my brain responding clearly, "We are going to open up our own private practice." I reacted like, "What? No, we're not. Where are you getting that thought?" I went home after that training, and the energy I had was off the charts. I kept sharing all my insights with my friend. I had so much energy! The burdens had been lifted.

I found other practitioners, and we formed the Midwest Brainspotting Institute. I opened up a private practice. This all happened within two years of the brainspotting training. I was envisioning this stuff, having these conversations with eight-year-old Cherie and future Cherie. I was having daily conversations with this eight-year-old and with future Cherie, asking myself, "What do we want to do?" and "Who do we want to be?"

I reminded myself that I was only in my 40s and had plenty of time ahead of me. My mentors were in their late 60s at the time, and my mindset was that if they could do it, then so could I. I just needed to figure out what I wanted, so I started having internal conversations with my younger self and my future self. This future me, by the way, was both exercising daily and being overall healthier. What an inspiration! I still talk with my parts daily, and my future self helps me with great marketing ideas!

Opportunity

I began intentionally envisioning while on a brainspot, and I did that every morning for a while. I started seeing all these opportunities, and my fears began to ease away. I told my husband that I wanted to open my own private practice. He asked me how we were going to do that, and I couldn't give him an answer. Yet.

I suggested maybe a loan, but we couldn't afford it alone. I didn't know how I was going to make it happen, but I was determined. I had a dream one night, not long after, and in my dream, it said to seek help from women business owners.

Intrigued, the next morning I typed in "Women entrepreneurs who help other women entrepreneurs…"

This led me to E&S Advisors. I was getting stuck in my business plan phase. Specifically, the SWOT analysis you have to do in order to show your business can make a profit. I was a woman. This was for me. I need support to finalize a business plan. I had written up a business plan, but I couldn't do the rest on my own.

We met the women from E&S Advisors at a coffeehouse. I explained what I wanted, and they said, "Okay, it's going to cost around $5,000."

I didn't have that kind of money in my savings, but what I did have was a tiny bit of wiggle room. On a tight budget ourselves, my husband and I each had a personal allowance of $200 from our household funds for socializing. I asked the women if they would be willing to take my allowance as payment toward the business plan, and we could write the rest of the funds into the business loan when they helped me get it.

They agreed! I was excited, and we spent six months creating an ironclad business plan. My husband and I paid off a bunch of debt. I worked hard to pay it off, so I only had to make about $900 a month for the next year.

The first bank we visited was Associated Bank, a large bank with branches worldwide. A young kid, who looked to be about 18, sat down with me, sighing. Uh oh. I said, "Did you draw the short straw? You're going to tell me it's a no, right?"

He started to respond, but I cut him off, "Did you even read my proposal?"

He blushed; it was clear he was embarrassed. I said, "That's okay. If you can't see the seriousness of this and how I'm going to impact the community, I don't want to work with your bank."

I got up and left. I was absolutely heartbroken. My new business advisors, Susan and Beth, tried to comfort me. Susan said, "Don't worry, don't worry. There are other banks."

I was hesitant, but we went to Nicolet National Bank next with Susan. This was a smaller, community-oriented bank, which initially put me in a somewhat discouraged attitude. This time, Susan's sitting down with me, across from two young guys. I was like, "Oh God."

But these two young men surprised me; they were in their 30s and started asking me educated questions about my business plan.

I was happy to know they actually read it, and they were even telling me how it was going to be so good for the community when it started. I was flattered but taken aback. I said, "What do you mean *when* this starts?"

One of the young men goes, "Well, we're giving you the loan."

I was shocked. I even get emotional now thinking about it, but I couldn't believe this was happening. It was a moment where I felt someone really believed in me. Someone listened to my ideas and was very encouraging.

I tried to stay calm; then Susan and I went out into the parking lot to take everything in. This was a $40,000 loan, plus the money we were investing from our retirement. Our in-laws gave us a gift, and with that, the total investment came to about $90,000. I can't remember all the figures, but I know it was a big amount because it was freaking me out. I had to do this now. I need to establish a private practice mental health clinic to serve my community. While it was all a bit nerve-wracking, I was elated. The money was coming together.

We were in the parking lot, jumping up and down. I was thrilled, but I also had business to attend to! Realizations started to hit me. I was like, "Oh my God, I gotta find a place to rent. I gotta get computers, and I've gotta work within this budget."

Within two years, I had 11 employees and the business loan had all been paid off.

All from daily self-spotting with little Cherie and my future Cherie. Visioning what I wanted. Get Connected Counseling and Consulting was about connection, community, and awakening people. That has always been the core message.

After that happened, I was like, "Well, if I can do this, what *else* can I do?"

That's when I started thinking about David Grand and my desire to become a trainer. Part of becoming a trainer back in the day was to follow other trainers around at their trainings, so I could learn what they did and how to teach. I didn't have the money to be going all over the place, but I didn't let this stop me.

I got another business loan. I had paid off the first one, so the bank readily approved another loan. After I became a trainer, I didn't make a profit for about six years because I was going around and learning as much as I could. Driving around to these small towns in the Midwest, educating people about brainspotting. Some of my training sessions were only with six people, but that's how it began.

One day, David said to me, "You've got to think internationally. I want you to fly overseas, come to Brazil, and present on how you use brainspotting with couples."

I didn't like flying; I preferred driving around the Midwest. He encouraged me to use brainspotting before making a decision, so I did. At the time, I had just taken on a business partner who became the clinic manager, which gave me more flexibility. With that support, I began traveling more, and I eventually overcame my fear of flying. This was only possible through all of the brainspotting work I had been doing.

Two things happened simultaneously when I was going to Brazil. One, my business partner came to me and said, "I can't do this anymore," after a year and a half of being a business partner. We had a five-year plan and a ten-year plan, and we had already agreed that if we wanted to go in different directions, we would honor that in each other. She wasn't happy, and she needed to leave; the right people will never hold that against you. I am glad that we had discussed this possibility beforehand. We are still friends today.

After she shared this with me, I had to decide what to do with the clinic. I couldn't be there all the time managing it because I was traveling and teaching. I had to dip into my savings because some of the clinicians I had there weren't retaining clients. I would discuss it with them, but nothing changed.

Additionally, I was going to Brazil at the same time as some of the clinicians in my practice. I shared with them that the clinic couldn't afford to have the three practitioners gone at the same time, but they decided they were going to go anyway..

I wasn't sure how to problem-solve this situation at first; the people-pleaser part of me was still there, wanting to take care of everyone. I decided to go to everybody to talk to them, and I realized that a lot of them didn't have any skin in the game. I was the one taking care of everyone's burdens, and nobody seemed to care about mine. They thought I was making money hand over fist, which I was not.

Because a few of them were not retaining clients, I was actually going into my savings to keep the clinic open. That is when I realized this was no longer sustainable and did not align with what I wanted to continue doing in the brainspotting community. I realized I was not aligned with my values. I also realized this was a pattern in my life. I was looking for the family I never had. I was trying to create a community of connection, but I was stuck in people-pleasing mode. I also realized how much I prioritize the care of others at the expense of my own needs. These were patterns I needed to break.

I decided to close the clinic. I invited the folks who wanted to stay to open their own private practices, I could help them, and then we could form a group collective. This way, everyone had equal skin in the game. I could teach and travel without being responsible for everyone. We could support each other and rise together. This was more aligned with my values.

I agreed to provide the services they need to learn how to open their own private practices. They would have to pay for these services. For example, I could teach them how to open an LLC, best billing practices, and successful marketing strategies.

After that, the number of people quickly dwindled, but I ended up with four who stuck around. I taught them how to open up their own private practice, and that lasted for about three or four years.

I did the same pattern with the collective that I did with my employees. I was overly helpful and generous, again trying to build a connected community in place of the one I did not have. Again, it was at my expense. Another pattern emerged during this time. I set a boundary, and the whole group decided to leave.

Now, I could have told myself a story about how I was betrayed after doing so much for everyone. Instead, I accepted what happened and reframed this moment as setting a boundary to take care of myself. I was learning. This is how people get weeded out of your life. As you grow and change, the right people will come through the door, as I open it up to other opportunities and people who are more aligned and authentic. They say what they mean and mean what they say. Their behavior also matches what they say. This is how I have learned to discern who I would like in my inner circle. People like that are important to me, especially after my lived experiences.

I had previously shared with the group that it was important to me not to be the last to know if something was being said about me. We had agreed to use dialogue to address any concerns that might arise as a group, and everyone was on board with that approach. We had all received training in having open, respectful conversations, especially around difficult topics.

Even with that agreement in place, I later sensed that conversations were happening that I wasn't part of. No one had come to me directly, but I could feel a shift. My assistant at the time confirmed to me that she had heard people talking about me and that they had concerns. At a group meeting, I gently acknowledged what I was picking up on and said, "I have a sense that something is being discussed, and I want to name it." At that moment, it was met with denial.

About two weeks later, the therapists presented a proposal outlining the changes they wanted me to make. After reflecting on it, I realized that what they were asking would have hurt my business, so I declined. That's when they told me they planned to leave. One of them paused and said, "You were right. I want to own that. We were talking about you. It was hard to come directly to you because you are intimidating."

I responded with genuine curiosity, "I appreciate your honesty. But I'm confused, because we all have the same training in dialogue. We agreed to resolve any conflicts through open and constructive dialogue. I would have welcomed the opportunity for an open conversation." This was another experience of learning to let go for me. This one really hurt. After that meeting, they all decided to leave and did not talk to me during their departure. They all moved to the other side of the building together. I continued to say hello in the bathroom as our office space shared the bathroom.

I began to reframe the experience inside myself through the lens of manifestation, focusing not on what had gone wrong but on what I truly desired in my life. I realized I wanted to surround myself with people of integrity, those who show up with honesty, respect, and a willingness to share the load. I wanted relationships built on mutual effort and reciprocity, where I'm not the only one holding responsibility. I wanted people in my life who could navigate conflict and have difficult conversations.

And now, that's exactly who I have in my life.

The people around me are here not just to receive, but to contribute as well. They value the connection as much as I do. But I understand that I had to go through those earlier challenges to gain clarity. Those experiences helped me see the contrast and taught me what I genuinely needed and deserved in my relationships. I share all of this in the hope that if you have had some of these experiences, you, too, can understand that some of these experiences are based on the trauma lens you hold. Over time, as you learn about your patterns and adjust them, your perception of the world and your experiences in relationships can change.

Going through that gave me the courage to say, "No, you're not going to treat me like that." This experience helped me recognize my worth and gave me the confidence to set and express my boundaries. Again, this was all happening as I was brainspotting and self-spotting. I was talking to that eight-year-old and future Cherie, working through internal guilt and shame. I wanted to have good endings with everybody, but that didn't always happen. Through this work, I have gained a deeper understanding, and I'm very happy with my current life. I needed to be on my own for a bit. It was important for me to know that I can value myself and that it's okay if I have solitude.

Where We Are Today

Amidst the darkness that surrounds us in the world today, I felt a deep calling to create something that shines with light and hope. I want people to know that healing is possible, even when the voices around us say otherwise. From that vision, the Mindful Co-Regulation Training was born, and the Elevated Life Academy emerged, both serving as beacons of inspiration, resilience, and renewal.

Ten years into our marriage, my spouse and I knew we were in trouble. We often fought without ever finding a resolution. I came from a family that yelled; he came from a family that kept their feelings locked inside. Neither of us knew how to stay connected when conflict arose.

Our first breakthrough came when we finally learned how to dialogue. This allowed us to truly hear each other and begin practicing co-regulation. But even with these tools, something was still missing. Over time, we realized we were acting out our unhealed traumas on each other, making it hard, sometimes impossible, to stay connected. We were hurting each other in ways we didn't fully understand.

That's when we added brainspotting to our dialogue coaching sessions. This allowed us to go deeper and release old hurts from the early years of our marriage. I had PTSD, something I didn't recognize at the time, and I was highly reactive. Paul, meanwhile, flirted with substance abuse. We often fell into power struggles, unable to truly appreciate one another.

Going even deeper, we then incorporated parts work. I discovered younger parts of myself that were deeply wounded and mistrustful of Paul. He realized that parts of him, shaped by being bullied as a child, were easily triggered during our arguments.

Stacking the approaches of dialogue, brainspotting, and parts work has transformed our relationship. It saved our marriage.

Today, this integrated method has become the foundation of *Mindful Co-regulation in Relationships*, a training I now share with healers worldwide (Lindberg, 2025). It is a blessing to see these tools save not only marriages, but also friendships, families, and connections of every kind.

As I continued to grow in my business, I asked myself a simple but powerful question: How can I keep sharing the message that you, too, can live an elevated life?

I believe that with the right tools and support, anyone can shift their perspective on themselves and others, and that shift can change everything. But I also knew that not everyone can afford counseling. I wanted to ensure that important, life-changing information was available to everyone, regardless of their circumstances.

That's how Elevated Life Academy was born.

Elevated Life Academy is a heart-centered, community-based platform built on the belief that healing and growth should be accessible. We offer free resources, inspiring conversations on our podcast, and educational opportunities for healers, including trainings with continuing education (CE) credits.

At its core, Elevated Life Academy is about giving back, lifting others up, and creating a space where transformation is possible for anyone ready to step into their full potential. It's slow going, but it's there. We're still working on it. The podcast has been running smoothly for over a year. I wanted it to be focused on, like your typical healer, and real-life stories of healers all over the world. We just completed a women's entrepreneur series. All these young women in their 20s who are single mothers now have their own private practices. We discussed how to balance it and talked about their manifestation process. It's been incredibly inspiring.

Real Experiences

I have contacted two authors for the podcast. First, there is James Doty, who wrote *Mind Magic*. He's a neuroscientist who discusses how manifesting is a real phenomenon (Doty, 2024). Then, there is Dr. Sabrina Brennan, author of the *Neuroscience of Manifesting* (Brennan, 2024). She's from Ireland and absolutely amazing. She was a quick responder and has already been on the podcast. I'm still working on getting James Doty on a future episode because his ideas are deeply connected to spirituality.

When I started to manifest, these spiritual experiences began to occur. People started to ask, "Well, how are you doing this?" I just started talking about all these daily practices; grit, resilience, learning about flow states, and perseverance help me get through it all.

Then, Heather Corbet and I created the "Brainspotting, Spirituality, and Intuition" training. We discuss all of this and teach daily practices to help you achieve your goals. We came up with a tagline, "Putting the science in the woo", because as we've discussed, people tend to assume, "Oh, that's woo-woo" when you talk about spirituality or manifesting.

There's real science behind this, and it's time to bring it into the spotlight. By practicing consistently, repeating new patterns, and tapping into flow states, we can actually rewire our behavior in the world. When we practice, we improve, and our brains become trained.

I didn't realize it at the time, but that's exactly what I was doing all those years, training myself, step by step, to live differently.

Now, I feel called to share what I've learned. I want to teach others how to access this way of being, because I deeply believe everyone deserves the chance to live their dreams and experience what's truly possible.

Everyone can do this! You have to put in the self-work; it's not something that just comes to you. Some of us are lucky enough to have it easier, but most of us need hard work, persistence, determination, and repetition. This is how the brain and central nervous system get rewired.

Through these practices I connected with my eight-year-old self, which helped me remember that she had wanted to be an actress. She had so much creative energy! Reconnecting with that energy reminded me of my big dreams and, more importantly, that I can accomplish great things. I was starting to believe it. Eight-year-old Cherie wanted to be out there and entertain people. She's very inspiring.

Intention

At the same time that I was beginning to feel burnt out from traveling, deep trauma therapy work, and supporting clients with intense levels of dissociation, life delivered another blow: my best friend, Kim, passed away, and my father got cancer for the second time.

The very next day, something shifted inside me. It was as if my brain whispered, "We're done with trauma work."

I knew it was time for a new chapter, one focused on post-traumatic growth, high performance, and rediscovering joy. I had a clear vision, a spiritual message guiding me to go for it. Within three months, I made the bold decision to close my psychotherapy practice and rebrand as a coaching practice under my own name: Cherie Lindberg, LLC. All of this happened while I was still completing my doctorate. It was a lot, but I was never alone.

Thankfully, I have an incredibly supportive husband, Paul, who stood beside me through it all. It wasn't easy at first. There were moments of doubt, after all, I had spent a lifetime building my education, and now I was pivoting in a completely new direction. At times, we both were fearful of facing change. Living into uncertainty is not for the faint of heart.

However, once Cherie Lindberg, LLC was fully launched, the vision for Elevated Life Academy came into focus with clarity and purpose.

Then, I hit the ground running, informing all my clients that my therapy practice would be closing in three months. I went to my webmaster, and they helped me rebrand my site to focus on coaching. In those three months,

I took a flow coaching class and a parts coaching class to gain the transition skills I needed. I rebranded and started sharing with people what I was doing.

All the professional people wanted me to coach them. They said, "I want you to help me get where you're at." So, we started creating these conscious action plans that ask, "Okay, what do you want?" It's all driven by intention, daily practices, and taking action. We reverse-engineered their plans and started to brainspot any barriers. We often ended up going deeper with brainspotting and parts work to understand the blocks that were deep..

That's the big problem: people see their dreams, and maybe they feel them, but they don't change their behavior or take action to achieve them. I often discuss habit formation and changing habits with people. You won't get what you want if you don't put in the effort. In fact, I just recently had a couple who struggled with this. I'd been working with them for two months, and they were not doing the things I was asking. It is challenging to establish new habits when old ones are deeply ingrained.

However, we can get there little by little. You do not have to do it alone. Get a coach. Get a therapist. Find the support you need.

I looked at both of them and said, "You are paying me good money each hour you are here. You're not getting the results you need because you are not practicing. I can't make you do it. You have to choose: do you really want what you say you want? Look at it. Because if you do, you're going to have to change your habits."

Many people have the misconception that change will happen miraculously, and I am happy to take their money, but I don't want to waste anyone's time, or my time for that matter.

People invest time and money, but ultimately, it comes down to changing ingrained habits and following the guidance they are given. One step at a time. Rebuilding is a process. You may have years of habits that you need to rework and reprocess. Many folks are on autopilot. I want people to see results. It's a matter of what is getting in the way. I hear things like, "Well, he should do this," or "she shouldn't do that." That won't go anywhere.

I encourage clients to "let it begin with you."

It's got to begin with you, inside. We can't change another person. We have to be willing to change ourselves. To this couple in particular, I said, "You deserve to have the relationship of your dreams, but that doesn't come in a cracker jack box. It comes from doing the work and living your intentions one day at a time."

Everything I share, I actively practice in my own life. I'm far from perfect, but my husband and I are intentional about nurturing our relationship. We do check-ins twice a week and set aside time each month for our coaching appointment to help us stay conscious and connected. It's part of how we continually shape the kind of relationship we both want to experience.

We believe that relationships are the foundation of a meaningful life. They help us feel safe, seen, and loved—and they create the space where deep healing can truly happen. Paul has held space for some of my most tender, wounded parts, and I hope he would say I've done the same for him.

We returned from Costa Rica this past February, where we made the time to invest in each other. That's what it takes: presence, care, and a shared commitment to growing together.

Back to the couple, I tried taking a creative approach. This young gentleman said to me, "Left to my own devices, I wouldn't do any of this stuff. Like, it doesn't make sense." I attempted to speak to his logical side. He's a budget guy, and I drew a connection between budgeting and psychology; you can't take more out than what you're putting in. I told him he had to nurture the connection; otherwise, distance gets created, and that's when divorce happens.

You get to decide what you want to nurture here. You either want to nurture a connection or distance; it's up to you. You need perseverance and determination. Do what you say you're going to do; we can call it this magic word: *manifesting*. You manifest through your actions and intentions. You take action, and this is how our dreams really do come true. One step at a time!

Struggling with Mediumship Gifts

I've got a part that comes in and thinks too much when I am getting messages from those who have passed. Spirit is really smart, and what Spirit's been doing is kind of sneaking a reading up on me. Not too long ago, during a casual conversation with an attendee at the Costa Rica intensive, we sat down together and, almost immediately, I felt the presence of a male standing on my right side. I said her name, and before I could say another word, she asked, "He's here, isn't he?"

She began to share her story. She had met him in treatment, and they eventually married. As she continued to heal, he continued to relapse. Finally, she filed for divorce.

On his birthday, he chose to end his life in the driveway of the home they had once shared. She wasn't there that night; something in her intuition had told her not to go home. Later, she learned what had happened and discovered he had left behind a journal meticulously detailing his plans, along with other papers and pieces of jewelry.

What struck me was that he had tried to contact her a year earlier at this very retreat center with another medium. At that time, she had said no. This time, she was ready. His message was clear; he was asking for forgiveness. She told me she did not hold a grudge.

Then, he shared something more with me: it was time for her to let go of the things of his she had kept. When I asked, she admitted she still had the journal, the papers, and some jewelry. She explained that she had held onto them because she feared people might not believe her story. But he was urging her to release them, not out of shame, but as an act of freedom. On some level, he was trying to make amends, to lift the lingering weight these objects carried in her life.

I gently shared that it felt important for her to release that energy. After returning home from Costa Rica, she sent me a video of herself throwing the items into a river. She told me it felt like a profound release, like a door had finally closed, allowing her to step fully into the next chapter of her life.

When I have these experiences with a soul coming in wanting me to share something with their loved one, I often have thoughts of, "Oh, that was made up," or "That was fake," or whatever, but it in this case it really resonated with her. I have to admit that I saw her receive healing from that experience. I saw her experience it physically, and this made me realize I could help people heal if I were open to sharing these experiences. After these experiences and many more, I decided to explore my psychic gifts and mediumship further. It was also around this time I began to delve deeper into manifestation.

You can self-spot and open yourself up to your gifts; you just have to be curious and let yourself believe! This is hard as culture has programmed us to look for science or proof! Our culture often shuts others down, shames them, or blames them when their beliefs do not align with our own. I am realizing that acceptance is the key to unlocking your mediumship gifts. And I know this can help other people. I can personally tell when I'm channeling or when spirit is talking to me; my body feels different. Interestingly, it's coming from Spirit right now. My brain said, "Okay, look up, you're on the spot right here." This is the key to how you manifest and open up to your mediumship gifts. I have mediumship spots that open me up to messages.

If you can self-spot, you already possess the abilities that support mediumship. It's a powerful skill that allows you to connect deeply—not only with yourself but with others. I say this with confidence because self-spotting has supported me in every area of my life. It is the programmed part of our brain that we need to bypass in order to access deeper levels of consciousness.

These spots act as portals into the universal field of information. They open pathways to insight, healing, and connection. That's why developing a daily practice isn't just helpful—it's essential. It reinforces your ability to stay tuned in and aligned with your higher guidance.

Practical Application of Manifestation

First, take a moment to clarify what you want to invite into your life. What do you truly desire? This step can be challenging for some; often, we're much more aware of what we *don't* want than what we do. But don't let that stop you. Simply reflect without pressure or judgment.

For example, I'm currently working intentionally to manifest healing in my ancestral line. That's something I'm deeply committed to. At the same time, I'm calling in greater abundance, both in my personal life and in my business. On one hand, I'm doing deep healing work. On the other hand, I'm creating space for expansion and growth.

So ask yourself: What do you want to experience more of? Can you picture it? Can you sense what it might be like in your body: peaceful, energized, free, and grounded?

Let that vision guide you. That's where the magic begins. Feel into this desired outcome, embody it, then anchor it in with a brainspot!

This is where many people get stuck. They think they feel a block in their body, but sometimes we have to process the block to envision and embody what we want. With practice, we become increasingly adept at opening ourselves to possibility.

Go out and look at the world around you as well. Inspiration is everywhere! Who do you admire, read, or listen to? What inspires you? If you feel inspired, that's your body saying "yes" to something. Follow the energy!

We can do some self-spotting to increase the "yes" or the inspiration. Sometimes that's going to show up in a part of you, and sometimes it'll show up through a body sensation, vision, or an image. You must practice with it every day to anchor it into your physiology, so look for any opportunity to access it. You're going to get more images and details when you do that because the more you practice, the more your brain's creative power is going to open up and show you the way.

I find that if I feel a "yes" in my stomach, for instance, I'll look for a spot where that feeling is particularly strong, and then I'll practice with it daily. I'm going to write it down in my journal and tell other people about it. All those different things create that practice, and you're putting it out there and reinforcing it inside. Sometimes, I have experienced this by pretending I already have it, noticing what that feels like, and anchoring that feeling in.

I want to emphasize: practice the "yes", practice the inspiration, and ground it in your physiology, and then take action.

The action is to keep practicing, feel it, gain confidence, and then take the next step to realizing it.

Manifestation feels like a resonance, helping your brain and neurons connect with new opportunities that align with them. This will help you with discernment and what to and what not to say "yes" to. It's almost like we're programming ourselves for the good and reprogramming ourselves to our desires.

In September 2024, I led a group trip to Scotland. Before we even traveled, I had brainspotted everything! I had seen myself on that bus, watching people take in the sights and explore castles. Before any of it became a reality, I had to figure out how to make it happen. I began researching logistics, contacted a travel agent, and outlined all the necessary steps.

I found others who really wanted to come along, and one gentleman on the trip had even told me he had never taken two full weeks off work before. Now he's got the travel bug. He's like, "Yes, I recommend everybody do it at least once a year when you can, so that you can see other parts of the world."

Manifesting Your Life

You really *can* manifest big things. My PhD is one of the most significant examples in my life. Yes, I put in the work, but it was also a clear manifestation of my efforts. I had a deep desire to write a book, and I knew that having a PhD after my name would give it more credibility and reach than just my professional license. The book was always the end goal, and getting a PhD was the step that made the most sense to support it.

A PhD typically costs around $80,000 and takes approximately six years to complete. I found an online program that offered academic PhDs—not clinical ones, meaning I couldn't become a licensed psychologist through it, but that was never the point. I already make more than most psychologists. This wasn't about income. It was personal. I wanted to prove to *myself* that I could design and complete a research study and contribute to brainspotting.

Throughout the journey, I utilized brainspotting to process the insecurities that arose. I had no idea how I would pay for the program at first. But deep down, I knew something important about myself: if I didn't fully commit up front, I might talk myself out of it. So, I took a leap and secured a business loan to pay for it in full. And that decision changed everything.

My best friend, a colleague, and my dad all had cancer at the same time. I was working full-time, running a business, and traveling the world. I felt like a mountain climber with a rope around my waist, and somehow, something kept pulling me forward. I never imagined I would actually complete it. The cherry on top of everything is that I was going through menopause and dealing with COVID. The brain fog was real, and this was one of the hardest things I've ever done. But I invested in support to help me through it, and I made it. I'm so glad I pushed through!

Manifestation isn't about just wishing for something; it's about committing fully, taking consistent action, and trusting the process, even when the path feels uncertain or impossible. It takes grit. Every challenge I faced tested my self-confidence, but I kept moving forward. That's the real power of manifestation: when you set a clear intention and refuse to give up, the universe begins to meet you with unexpected opportunities.

This journey also became another powerful opportunity to weed people out of my life, those who questioned my vision or made me doubt myself. Some said, "You're crazy," or asked, "Why would you do that? Aren't you in your 50s? Shouldn't you be thinking about retirement?"

However, I knew that to reach this goal, I needed to be surrounded by an encouraging and inspiring energy. I had to discern, once again, who I allowed into my space. I needed people who lifted me up, not drained me.

I didn't accomplish any of this on my own. My support system was everything. My friends and my husband were the wind beneath my wings, listening to my worries and reminding me of my strength when I momentarily lost sight of it. Their belief in me fueled my own.

CHAPTER 7

Discernment

Discernment involves having a reciprocal relationship with someone, where you carefully evaluate the advice you receive and determine how applicable it is to your life. You don't take every piece of advice that crosses your path, even from someone admirable and respectable.

My discernment journey has been primarily shaped by mentorship, and, unfortunately, through some painful experiences of betrayal. Because of this, I approach mentorship with a focus on both guiding others and choosing the right mentor for myself.

When seeking a mentor, start by identifying who truly resonates with you. Pay attention to the people you feel a natural connection with, but don't stop there. Observe them; do they follow through on their words? Are their actions aligned with what they teach? Many individuals have the potential to connect, but true mentorship requires integrity. If someone's behavior doesn't match their words, that's a relationship that requires discernment.

Discernment has played a significant role in many of my relationships, from those I mentor to those who mentor me. Not every mentor or relationship will be the right fit for my journey, and that's okay. Discernment allows me to recognize who will genuinely support me and who truly resonates with my path. In turn, this helps me offer the same level of support to others, as we connect at a meaningful point in our journeys.

I seek mentors who reflect my aspirations. The saying "practice what you preach" resonates because that's what a good role model is meant to do!

I try to follow this principle and encourage others to do the same. Discernment is about role modeling wisdom and sharing, fostering equal learning within the mentor-mentee relationship. I've learned just as much from my mentees as they have from me, making it a truly reciprocal and supportive experience.

Not everyone approaches mentorship this way. Many mentors view themselves as superior to their mentees; some mentees, in turn, idolize their mentors. For me, discernment is defined by a reciprocal relationship full of mutual support and growth.

I often say, take what you like and leave the rest. It's essential to foster openness and acceptance; you always have your own opinion, and the best mentors encourage independent thought and self-confidence.

Some advice will resonate with you, and some won't, and that's okay! A good mentor is never gonna say, "I know best and you follow me completely." That's where you're veering into some culty territory. Beware.

If you find yourself in this situation, it can be difficult to recognize at first. Often, we enter a stage of disillusionment, and when we start to wake up, we realize there's a misalignment and possibly even compliance going on in the relationship.

Maybe we had blind spots with someone, or perhaps we didn't fully trust ourselves. In these moments, it's easy to be hard on ourselves; I know because I've been there. I've been duped before, and it's painful to realize how much I let someone influence me and my self-concept.

There was one situation where this happened to me early in my life, and I was really proud of how I had handled it, despite the pain it caused me.

In my late 20s, early 30s, I was working on my co-dependency. I would meet monthly with a group of older women. The group was very confrontational, though at the time, I didn't see this as a bad thing. This was in the 90s, and many healing methods were confrontational and shaming then.

I thought confrontation was positive. They'd say things like "Well, I'm noticing this about you, Cherie, are you recognizing an underlying pattern here?" I thought that was a good thing because they were helping me catch my blind spots. They were also 20 years older than me, and I felt safe with them at the time because I genuinely believed they were mentoring me.

There was an older woman in the group who had started a new relationship. The rest of the group did not approve of this relationship, and I witnessed everyone shame her and accuse her of going back into a codependent relationship. I decided to speak out about how uncomfortable their shaming made me, and then they started to do it to me!

I said we should all be able to think for ourselves and trust ourselves, even if maybe we're making a mistake. We all have our own journeys to live. I told them there is a lesson to learn here, but they didn't listen. They just projected their shame onto me. I was honestly shocked. This caught me off guard. This all happened before email, so I wrote a very long letter to everybody and mailed it, saying goodbye to the group.

I said, "This no longer feels like mentorship, this no longer feels like a safe environment for me to be my own individual self. I wish you all well. But what you are doing here is shaming and blaming, highlighting character defects and the ego. We've all already been through this with our childhood trauma, and now we're replicating this in the group. I'm not going to have any part in this".

This group never spoke to me again. At the time, this was a hard season because I was already estranged from my mother and father, so their silence felt like another deep loss, like losing family all over again. It was yet another chapter in my search for a safe, supportive community that felt like *home*.

But looking back, I can see that I hadn't yet addressed the root of my people-pleasing pattern. I kept choosing friendships with people who weren't truly safe, hoping each time that things would be different. Still, I'm incredibly proud of the younger version of myself, young woman Cherie, who stood up for herself and for another person in that group. She chose alignment over approval, even when it was hard.

These women were two decades older than me, but I was the one who modeled a healthy boundary and said, "You will not treat me like this."

That moment brought up a mix of emotions, sadness for the loss, but also a deep sense of strength and integrity. Looking back now, I believe this was part of a much bigger lesson, possibly even a karmic one. As I mentioned in Chapter Five, my Human Design number shows that I'm here to be a role model. And to clear this pattern, I had to be the one to blaze the trail. I didn't realize it at the time, but this dynamic would repeat in my life for at least another decade. If you find yourself in a similar cycle, please don't be discouraged. Healing takes time. Growth unfolds layer by layer. The beautiful news? That pattern *has* been healed. And I'm a stronger, more whole person because of it.

When mentoring someone or choosing the right mentor, the first thing I consider is whether they truly resonate with me and align with my values. Consider asking yourself these kinds of questions, but the answers aren't always easy to discern. Discernment can be difficult! Many mentors contradict themselves by saying one thing and doing another.

When a mentor's words don't match their actions, it becomes a form of propaganda. Some say what they think will resonate with others, but their actions tell a different story. When people are in a vulnerable place and seeking hope, they can easily get hurt. This is why I get so angry; people are taken advantage of, experience trauma, and suffer under the guidance of a leader simply because they didn't take a moment to pause and discern.

I've experienced this myself. I've had to evaluate and filter through advice, deciding what truly aligns with me. Just because something worked for my mentor doesn't mean it's the right path for me. Does it resonate with where I want to go? Does it fit my journey? A mentor is there to provide guidance, but at the end of the day, it's up to you to self-reflect and make the right decision for yourself.

A Practical Process for Discernment

When seeking mentorship, start by defining your goals. What do you hope to gain from the relationship? Once you have those answers, write what you hope to achieve and observe your mentor closely. Do they say what they mean, and do they mean what they say? Discern for yourself if their words and actions are aligned. Pay close attention to how they handle challenges and conflict. If your mentor triggers you and addressing it leads to defensiveness rather than constructive dialogue, that's a red flag!

As you build the relationship, question how this person resonates with you. A great mentor encourages your growth and wants to see you rise and move beyond them.

Remember, mentorship is a fluid process, so do not take it personally when people come and go. In fact, if a mentor takes your departure personally, that's an indication they do not want to see you at your full potential. Instead of dwelling on it, be grateful for the experience and move forward.

Mentorship

Mentors play a valuable role; they're here to support reflection, growth, and expansion. However, it's also natural, and even healthy, for mentees to eventually outgrow their mentors. That's part of the journey. It's important to stay mindful, though. Sometimes, even well-meaning mentors can unintentionally limit their mentees' growth. This often happens, consciously or not, when a mentor resists the idea of someone surpassing them. The truth is, you can only evolve so far with one person.

I've witnessed this dynamic not only in the field of psychology but also within spiritual communities. That's why I always encourage people: not to make someone your guru.

Don't give your power away. Instead, turn inward. Trust your own inner guidance. That wisdom within you is your truest teacher.

In my experience, many mentees naturally form a close, nurturing connection with their mentor; it's part of the trust-building process. Over time, though, there comes a point when that dynamic needs to shift. I often say, with a bit of humor, "It's time to step into your independence," when I sense that a mentee no longer needs the same level of guidance. Part of healthy mentorship is knowing when to encourage someone to spread their wings. Growth involves eventually stepping out of the nest, and a good mentor recognizes and supports that process.

I have said to the folks that I mentor, "There will come a time when you'll surpass me, and that's exactly what's meant to be." At first, some resist the idea, but I reassure them: "That day will come, and I'll be genuinely happy for you." To me, that's what true mentorship looks like. Unfortunately, I've also seen situations where ego gets in the way, where a mentor might, consciously or not, undermine a mentee's confidence or create subtle doubt. That's why it's so important to regularly reflect and ask: *Do my mentor's values align with mine? Are their words consistent with their actions?* These are important questions that help ensure your growth remains supported, not stifled.

We don't want to blindly follow someone just because we like them. If discerning the right mentor feels tricky at first, that's completely okay; it takes time and experience. I've spent most of my life developing that skill, and along the way, I've experienced plenty of betrayal.

For a period, I found myself pulling back and closing off from others. Past experiences had made it difficult to discern who genuinely wanted to connect with *me* and who was more interested in what I could offer. As you grow in knowledge, experience, or visibility, it's natural for people to be drawn to that.

But sometimes, others' interest isn't in you personally; rather, it's about access or advancement. I've noticed that while many people are sincere and grounded, others have projected unrealistic expectations onto me, placing me on a pedestal or viewing me as someone who holds all the answers. In some cases, they've looked to me as a kind of "fixer" or guide to heal them completely. While I understand that this can stem from a place of hope or admiration, it's essential to remember that true connection is mutual and grounded in authenticity, not idealization.

I always tell people: Please don't put me, or anyone, on a pedestal because eventually, you'll be disappointed. Everyone is equally human. At some point, I'm going to say or do something that triggers you, and if you've idealized me, that illusion will come crashing down. That's why I have honest conversations with the people I mentor. I tell them I may be part of their entire journey, or I may only walk with them for a short time.

Shadow Sides

People can become very skilled at masking their shadow sides, a skill we often learn unconsciously as a way to stay safe in the culture in which we live. At some point, many of us adopt roles or masks, such as caretaker, helper, or performer, not out of malice, but as a way to feel worthy or protected.

There was once someone in my life. I had known her for many years. She was outgoing, generous, and often went out of her way to support others. Her nurturing nature made her easy to rely on, and she brought a sense of warmth to many interactions.

Then, one day, I set a clear boundary, something simple, respectful, and necessary. Just two days later, she abruptly cut ties with no explanation. After more than a decade of knowing one another, I was left stunned. I reached out, hoping for an open conversation and trying to understand her point of view, or at least repair the interaction, but she wasn't interested. That was our ending.

At first, I felt a deep sadness. I sensed she was reverting to a familiar pattern of people-pleasing, prioritizing harmony over honesty, and avoidance over growth. But I made a conscious choice not to label the situation as betrayal. I had shown up with integrity and care, and perhaps our souls had simply reached the end of their contract together. I came to learn an important lesson: not all relationships end with closure, and not everyone knows how to part ways with grace.

Sometimes, people need to create a story in which they're the "bad guy" just to justify their departure. That's not a reflection of your truth; it's a reflection of where they are in their journey.

Years later, she reappeared, as if nothing had happened. It was disorienting. I gently let her know that we couldn't move forward without first acknowledging what had taken place. When I discovered she was seeking a job, I knew I wasn't the right person to bring her back into my world in that way, but I was still able to support her by connecting her with someone else who valued her skills.

In the end, this experience taught me a great deal about boundaries, compassion, and the importance of discerning between someone's role and their readiness to do deeper work. Growth requires honesty, with ourselves and with others, and not everyone is ready to take that step. There are folks who will deflect and make it about you. It is so important to give yourself grace during these times. Check in with a trusted friend so you have support, too.

There are two ways we could take this. I could be bitter and view everything through a cynical lens, or I can acknowledge the fact that I showed up wholeheartedly. Despite everything, showing up through love resonates with my morals, values, and who I am as a person. I am proud of myself for that, but I know this is not somebody I'm going to have in my inner circle.

Moving forward from that, and other experiences entangled in that (mentioned in previous chapters), I promised myself I would never have another relationship that wasn't reciprocal.

Even to this day, within the last couple of years, I've been letting go of relationships that aren't reciprocal. I had to learn all of this the hard way, unfortunately, which is why I'm determined to share these lessons with you. We're all on this journey together, and we all experience losses at times. If I didn't lose all that, I wouldn't be at the awesome place I am at right now.

There are no regrets about what has been. Perhaps it could have happened better or unfolded more easily. I always wish for good endings, but I'm also only one side of the equation. I can't help others achieve a good ending if they don't know how to get there. I did my best with what I had at the time, and I know that in my heart.

Others, even you reading this book might think differently, and that's okay. We can have differences of opinion.

It's difficult to write so vulnerably, but if this helps somebody else out there, it's worth it. Being able to say no is about letting go and growing. Often, as you grow, you let go of something to reach the next stage of evolution. You must make room to evolve, and discernment is a crucial part of the growth process. In my personal reflection practice, I frequently journal. I connect with how I'm feeling and the way I observe things.

This helps me with my decision-making. When I mentor folks, I hear a lot about their grief. They struggle with letting go because, while grieving, they don't want to let go of what no longer serves them. They're afraid of going into uncertainty. It gets scary. That's why I always ask people if they truly want to grow. Growing means entering uncertainty repeatedly and letting go of things, which inevitably leads to loss.

You will find that as you grow, not everyone will evolve with you. I've had numerous mentors in my own life, only to find that I was duped. When something like this happens, it hurts so badly because you get so excited, thinking you've found the answer for yourself and feel part of something. But the only way out is through. I completely understand you want to take others with you so you do not have to be alone on the journey. However, we all have our own soul path. Some people are not meant to accompany us. We all have our own lessons to learn, which is why we are here.

Cultivate Through Discernment

When it comes to transparency and authenticity, you must cultivate that through your discernment. I ask for what I need, put it out there, and sometimes I get it, sometimes Spirit says no. When it comes to being truly authentic, someone might have a part of them that's scared of being transparent, fearing they'll lose something. So they hide.

This is where I have to trust my intuition. I'm meant to go through whatever these things are so that I can hear my lessons. I used to be surprised by people and their behavior, but I'm no longer. We are all different parts trying to evolve. There will be some people I vibe with and some people I don't, and that's ok.

I have a shadow side as well, and it is essential to remember that our parts can emerge at any point. This helped me let go of worrying about what other people think. That was one of my biggest fears, and I helped many therapists and healers with that. Being out on social media, I was afraid of being attacked or getting bullied. People troll, and they do nasty things, but with practice, I'm now much better at letting it go. We hear the saying, "Wounded people wound people." I have been wounded, and I have wounded too. This helps keep things in perspective for me. We are all on the crazy path called life.

We don't need to understand their behavior. We are the ones who get to decide what we tolerate and what we don't. I try to be compassionate and understanding, but there are some people out there who will express their pain because they don't know how to deal with it. They're judging others, and they're unaware that they're doing what was done to them. Unconscious living.

I do my best to lead with compassion, but that doesn't mean I'll tolerate repeated, hurtful behavior. I know my worth, and I won't allow anyone to diminish it. Holding onto truth means sometimes saying a firm "no" and making tough choices to protect my well-being.

For example, when you set a clear boundary and someone responds by ignoring your voice entirely or shutting you out of a conversation meant to be shared, take note. That's a red flag. Healthy relationships don't use silence or avoidance as a form of control or punishment.

If someone doesn't recognize how inappropriate that kind of behavior is, it's a sign they're not ready to be part of the inner circle. We all carry wounds, but we still have a responsibility to show up with respect. In my world, we face conflict with curiosity, communication, and care, not deflection or dismissal.

I had a religious person once write to me because she thought I was too democratic. I've never shared my politics, but I introduced myself with she/her pronouns and cared about inclusion. I had a slide discussing diversity, inclusion, and how trauma-informed care should be informed by diversity and inclusion. I received a horrible email instructing me on how to walk.

It takes a certain type of person who would take the time to go onto my website and write this very lengthy email on how I am worthless and how I should and shouldn't be. I just wrote her back and said this letter reflects more about her than it does me. Please don't contact me again. Some people just need to shit on other people because they are so self-righteous and they feel justified. It is terrible, and this keeps people small because they're so afraid of that happening. After turning 50, I've decided I don't put up with this crap anymore.

My Skeptic Lens

Just this week, while writing this book, I had my mentorship call with my psychic-mediumship mentor. He brought a guest on the call this week and asked me to take ten minutes to read to the guest on the call. That wasn't so bad, but after that, I was urged to get even more specific, and I could feel my panic. I had performance anxiety, which is so interesting because when I'm with brainspotting or I'm teaching, I don't usually experience any of that.

My mentor told me I did a great job. There's still a skeptic inside of me, and even though I read 99% of her accurately, there was still one "no". I was observing this inside myself, and the skeptic inside said there was no way this could be possible. This is important to note because many people believe you are born with a natural gift, and that is exactly what I thought as well. Everyone can cultivate these skills. Even though I got a "no" in this situation, the person I read said it was still related to her, just in a different way. Hey, I made an assumption!

Although the session was successful, we focused primarily on the psychic aspect rather than exploring the deeper meaning behind things. I was surprisingly accurate in what I sensed, but also deeply anxious. It was unsettling to see how clearly I was reading her, and at times, performance anxiety would blank out my mind completely.

Part of me was afraid to explore the deeper layers of meaning because I wasn't feeling a strong connection with Spirit, so I stayed with the facts and avoided the interpretation. Afterward, I was given some resources to study, which I've since been working through.

Later, I had a session with a trusted colleague who's also a medium. I shared all of this with her, and she held space for me while I used brainspotting to process what had come up. As I spoke, I became aware of perfectionistic parts rising within me, the parts that kept whispering, "You should be more connected to Spirit by now."

And then, something powerful happened. Each time I voiced a longing, such as "I wish I felt Spirit" or "I just need validation," I received something in return.

An image. A sensation. A knowing. Spirit *was* responding repeatedly. But my mind, filtered through the lens of skepticism, kept blocking the recognition. My colleague gently said, "Let me know when you're ready for my input."

When I was, she reflected back everything that had just occurred, direct evidence of the very connection I claimed I didn't have.

It was humbling. My own brain wasn't letting me see the truth that was unfolding in real time. I realized how strong our blind spots can be, and how easily we can get in our own way, even when the answers are right in front of us. Our brains have some strong programming. This experience brought up old trust wounds for me, wounds I'm still working through. It's an invitation to deepen my trust: in Spirit, in the intuitive messages I receive, and in myself. It's another layer of growth in my personal evolution. But here's the thing, this kind of growth isn't just for me. *Anyone* can develop this connection. These gifts are within all of us. It's simply a matter of whether we're open to them.

Our brains are far more powerful than we often realize, and neuroscientist Tara Swart shows this beautifully in her book *The Source: The Secrets of the Universe, the Science of the Brain* (Swart, 2019). She explains that the brain is not just for logic and problem-solving, but it also connects us to intuition, creativity, and a sense of higher purpose. By learning how to guide our thoughts and focus our intentions, we can rewire our brains in ways that help us heal, grow, and step into the lives we truly want to live. This blending of neuroscience and spirituality reminds us that we already possess the tools within us to create transformation.

Swart also has a new book forthcoming that promises to build on these ideas. While *The Source* introduced the concept of the brain as a gateway to transformation, her upcoming work is expected to go even deeper into how we can unlock this inner potential in practical and meaningful ways (Swart, 2019). Just as her first book bridged science and spirituality, her new book is anticipated to offer fresh insights for anyone wanting to live with greater purpose and connection.

As fate would have it, Tara Swart recently admitted in a podcast episode of The Diary of a CEO with Steven Bartlett (2025) that she's been in contact with her deceased husband. She ardently believes that strong emotions, such as grief, can heighten our senses, strengthening our connection with the natural and supernatural world, though she wouldn't call her connection with her husband's spirit paranormal. Instead, she considers it to be evidence of what the human consciousness is capable of once we let go of self-imposed limits and trust our senses. Drawing on her experience as a neuroscientist, she floated the possibility that there are actually many more than five senses, suggesting that there may be as many as thirty-four, and that some of these senses may influence how we perceive loss.

Even as I write this, knowing it will be shared in my book, I feel a sense of fear. Fear of being judged, of being dismissed, of being labeled as "woo." I know some colleagues roll their eyes at this kind of work. But often, that skepticism is rooted in their own unacknowledged experiences, ones they may not be ready to admit or explore. We are capable of expanding our consciousness. I believe these gifts are real. And if my willingness to use them can help others heal more deeply, then I'll keep showing up, despite the fear, despite the judgment. I share this because I know I'm not alone. Many people possess these gifts but keep them hidden out of fear. In a world that's quick to criticize what it doesn't understand, choosing to stand in your truth is an act of courage.

And to me, that courage is worth it.

_____

And in the end...

I know that I am living wholeheartedly and authentically. I am choosing to be burned again at some point. I've come to accept that this is part of my karmic journey here on Earth. I'm here to serve as a role model. I'm going to be the one to say it or do it and likely get burned. In the end, with all of these experiences and these pains, it created this constriction.

Through my personal work, I decided I am not going to live a constricted life. I'm going to live wholeheartedly, knowing I am living true to myself. I'm choosing to get burnt again, and I'm choosing that because I want to live freely. To the best of my ability, I'm living as authentically and genuinely as possible.

I realize I may be giving others material they could misuse, but living as my whole, authentic self is worth that risk.

Being fully me means I carry grief and pain at times, but life isn't only heavy. I also get to experience joy and play. They coexist.

As Brené Brown reminds us, "You can't have one without the other" (Brown, 2010).

Living Systems within
the Western Culture

Our culture is in a world of hurt right now, with more and more folks disconnected and traumatized. Often, I see people giving up. Hopeless.

All the things we're struggling with get in the way of our connections. Programmed beliefs can hinder authentic relationships.

Judgement rears its ugly head. People stigmatize others, both knowingly and unknowingly. There are many scared. Fearful. When people are in that mindset, they hurt others. They may not even be aware that they are reacting in this way, projecting their trauma and hurt onto other people.

Many are unaware of their impact. Many have lost their capacity for compassion toward others.

There are a lot of people walking around unconscious in our world. I think everyone needs nurturing and compassion, but also boundaries. When I travel, there are subtle things that show this. For example, the patriarchy.

There are especially things about the patriarchy that seem to come from an unconscious bias in this world.

Last time I was on an airplane, I was in the middle seat, which I absolutely hate. I avoid being in the middle seat as often as possible. This time, a man on each side took up more than their allotted space with what's been dubbed the "manspread". Just one, tiny, micro example of unconscious actions that stem from systems that favor one type of person over another.

Before I got off that plane, I saw another example of this. The plane landed, and the majority of the men stood up right away, jockeying for position to be out the door first.

Of course, not every man is like that. Many are well-raised, conscious people doing their best in the world. But even those dubbed "the good ones" can be unconscious in their actions.

It's often turned against us as women. If we stand up for ourselves, even if it's against a friend, we're not assertive or protective; we're a bossy bitch or whatever other unkind comments people can come up with. There are numerous derogatory names for women who are confident and empowered.

If a man stands up for himself, he's a leader. Yet when others do the same, they're often dismissed or stigmatized. At times, it feels as though we're moving backward as a society. I noticed this even as a child, and it extends far beyond gender roles.

People's ethnicity is used against them. Their learning styles or mental health differences are judged harshly. If someone doesn't learn in the way the system dictates, they're labeled as deficient. If they don't conform to the way Western culture dictates they should, they're devalued.

Difference is too often seen as a flaw. There was a moment when we began to finally embrace difference as a source of beauty and strength. But now, our culture threatens to slip back into viewing difference as something to be feared or diminished.

Just as things in our world seemed hopeful for expansion, it seems we will be going backwards. As a culture, we have not learned from our history. Things might have been getting better with the words neurodiverse and neurodivergent, but with all the cuts that are coming around the corner, folks who identify as neurodiverse will be marginalized again. We've reached a point where people no longer listen to research or heed our knowledge. We also do not honor intuition.

For example, much research in the world talks about how children would learn better if schools started later (Wheaton et al., 2016). Many children in rural areas start their day incredibly early, waking up as early as 5:00 a.m. to catch a 6:45 a.m. bus and arrive at school by 7:15 (Minges & Redeker, 2016).

Research consistently shows that when children and teens get the biologically necessary sleep provided by later school start times, they experience significant improvements in brain function, focus, emotional regulation, and many other areas of well-being. Additionally, studies emphasize the crucial role of a nourishing breakfast in preparing students for effective learning and emotional stability throughout the day.

For a time, some schools began listening to this research. School breakfast programs were put in schools, but under current administrative policies, much of that progress will be reversed. It's a stark example of how our systems often ignore the very knowledge we've already uncovered.

Instead, our societal structures remain shaped by outdated models that are divided and scheduled to serve capitalism and a narrow definition of progress. These systems are deeply ingrained. They feel immovable, largely because people adapt to them, unconsciously accepting routines and patterns of thought without ever pausing to question where they came from or whether they still serve us.

Our culture tends to have a way of encouraging compliance in exchange for convenience. Sacrificing community for a quick fix. When fear is activated, something our neurobiology is hardwired to respond to, most people default to survival mode. They go along, even when it's not ultimately in their best interest.

Those in power eagerly exploit this, tapping into our natural tendency to focus on threat and avoid risk. Our brains are hardwired toward negativity to help us survive. In turn, our Western culture systems are set up to exploit this.

The result is a population trained to obey rather than question, driven by the fear of exclusion and the pressure to appear normal. Our reactions and responses are often shaped by programming from our upbringing, community, and culture. Programming that rarely gets examined, let alone revised, in adulthood.

However, we can change that. Awareness is the first step.

By noticing our mental habits, questioning our inherited beliefs, and reconnecting with what the research (and our inner wisdom) tells us, we can begin to imagine and build systems that support health, equity, and actual progress. We need true leaders who represent our values, not our fears.

People must not lose the ability to question. As a nation, we must continue to encourage and sharpen critical thinking skills. The government, in particular capitalism, greed, consumerism, and the like, prefers followers. They don't necessarily want us to have our own opinions or to think for ourselves. This begins to restrict what can and can't be taught in schools. For example, I can't go teach personal growth in a graduate program for licensed social workers. Maybe one day…

In Western culture, new ideas, especially those related to trauma, are often overlooked, minimized, or misunderstood. Trauma is still something many people are uncomfortable talking about, and as a result, innovation in how we approach and treat it has been slow to gain traction. Meaningful change takes time, and it requires consistent voices and actions to challenge the status quo.

Within the mental health field, there are national organizations and governing bodies that shape the standards for licensed clinicians. These institutions, even the American Psychological Association, aka the APA, establish the benchmarks for what is considered truely evidence-based or what the gold standard is in treatment.

And yet, many of these standards have not fully integrated trauma-informed perspectives, particularly those that recognize the vital role of the body in healing.

It raises an important question: How can we provide effective care if the frameworks guiding our education and licensing remain heavily cognitive and overlook the body's wisdom? This isn't about pointing fingers, but recognizing that the systems in place reflect long-held beliefs and traditions that may no longer serve the complexities of modern clinical practice.

To move forward, we need a more holistic understanding, one that honors both the mind and the body. And that begins with reexamining the foundations of how we educate and empower healing professionals.

CBT and the Limits of the System

Cognitive Behavioral Therapy (CBT) has become one of the most widely recognized and recommended forms of therapy in the field of mental health. Designed to address present-day problems through structured strategies and solution-focused thinking, CBT has helped many people manage stress, anxiety, and other common challenges. For those dealing with day-to-day struggles, it can be incredibly effective and supportive.

However, when we begin to explore the full complexity of human psychology and neurobiology, especially in the context of trauma, CBT alone often does not go far enough. While it addresses thoughts and behaviors, it tends to bypass the deeper roots of trauma that are stored in the nervous system, particularly within the limbic system and subcortical areas of the brain. True healing from trauma often requires us to go beyond cognition and into the body, where unresolved experiences continue to live.

There is no one-size-fits-all approach to therapy. Yet our educational institutions and mental health systems often elevate certain modalities, such as CBT. These approaches neatly fit into the box that the mental health field has constructed.

Insurance companies often adopt the same criteria to decide whether a client can access the very services they need to heal, even though those clients are paying for coverage. In doing so, the industry itself can become a barrier to care, standing between people and the healing they deserve.

This is, in part, because CBT is structured, easy to research, and fits neatly within the frameworks required by insurance companies. These practical benefits are meaningful, but they also create limitations when it comes to supporting deeper emotional and somatic healing.

This gap and disconnection between what is taught in academic settings and what actually supports transformation and healing in the field is something many practitioners recognize. Modern neuroscience shows us that trauma lives in the body and brain in ways that talking alone cannot fully reach. Yet, practices that integrate somatic awareness, deeper brain-based approaches, or even spiritual frameworks are still met with skepticism or regulatory resistance in some professional circles.

Author and psychologist Dr. Lisa Miller, in her book *The Awakened Brain* (2022), explores this intersection of science and spirituality. Her research shows that a belief in something greater than oneself—regardless of what that belief is—can significantly buffer against depression, reduce the risk of addiction, and increase overall well-being. This highlights an essential truth: healing is not just a cognitive process. It is emotional, physiological, and often spiritual.

Unfortunately, spirituality is often misunderstood or avoided in clinical settings. Many practitioners shy away from addressing spiritual beliefs, sometimes confusing them with religion. While these can overlap for some, they are distinct from each other. Spirituality is a deeply personal aspect and can be an integral part of the healing process.

In some cases, even referencing the body-mind connection in therapeutic work—without a specific academic rationale—can lead to challenges in obtaining continuing education approval. This points to a broader issue: the therapeutic systems we work within often lag behind the evolving science of healing.

As practitioners and seekers, we are called to hold a wider view. One that honors the mind, the body, and the spirit. Moreover, while working within the system is often necessary, we must also be willing to question its limits and continue advocating for more integrative, trauma-informed approaches to care.

Yes. I have seen it happen, and that's part of why I created Elevated Life. I'm getting CEs. Our organization was connected to another organization that lost its CEs, and part of that is because they brought in a new board that was not trauma-informed, claiming that body therapies are not evidence-based, and blocking research funding.

Additionally, the popular researchers receive the majority of the research—a high percentage of which is male—and everyone has to compete for research funding. You also have to work for a university. With the current climate, there will be even fewer resources available. Folks like myself don't have a prayer of getting the money and research teams because I don't have the administrative power to do any of that stuff.

More and more people are turning to functional medicine and holistic practices—not because these approaches are trendy, but because they're recognizing that the traditional medical model isn't always delivering the healing they need. In some cases, medications may help, but in many others, they can simply numb symptoms without addressing the root cause. This creates a growing disconnect between what's available and how people actually heal.

While a diagnosis can be validating and useful for some, it can also carry unintended consequences. The Western medical model often frames mental health conditions primarily as chemical imbalances and disorders, rather than exploring them through the lens of trauma, lived experience, or environmental context. This limited view can make it harder for people to see the full picture of their healing journey.

Additionally, a diagnosis can become a double-edged sword. Some individuals find empowerment in naming what they're experiencing. It helps them make sense of their internal world and seek the support they need.

But others may begin to internalize the label, making it part of their identity in a way that can feel limiting or stigmatizing. And society often responds accordingly. Sometimes with compassion, but other times with restriction or judgment.

It's important to recognize that this isn't a one-size-fits-all conversation. For example, in our current system, a mental health diagnosis can even affect someone's ability to access life insurance. This raises deeper questions about how our society profits from physical and mental well-being and whether such structures are truly designed to support healing.

There have been lawsuits against insurance companies accused of placing profit over care, creating unnecessary barriers for people trying to access the support they need. These systemic issues highlight a broader cultural challenge: the influence of greed and profit-driven motives in spaces intended to serve health and healing.

The pharmaceutical industry, too, profits enormously from the mental health field, particularly through the expansion of diagnostic categories and long-term medication use. And all of this exists within a larger system that often overlooks the social, relational, and environmental factors that deeply influence mental health.

Ultimately, true healing requires us to look beyond symptom management. It invites us to explore the whole person, their history, context, relationships, and internal world. And that means reimagining a system that prioritizes integration over separation, care over profit, and healing over habit. I know I am idealizing here. But one day…

The disconnects can seem endless. I easily get frustrated with the mundane. But it all boils down to this: The majority of people are unconscious in their daily lives. They have lost their power. They have a fear response, and don't even realize that they're automatically reacting. However, the more someone does their personal work, the more conscious and empowered they become. People are existing, they aren't really living. All of this connects back to why I wanted to write this book in the first place: to help people.

It is not easy to take the power back. It is a daily practice made up of hundreds of thousands of tiny decisions and habits you form. You have to change the way you think, your habits, and the way you live. It's slow and mind-boggling and confusing and strange. To unpack the fact that the way you think has been indoctrinated into you and downloaded by generation after generation. That's not an easy thing to undo! So important for you to know you are not alone! There are many of us on this path of healing, growing, and evolving. Find your people and get support.

Changing your mindset comes first; then, you must change your daily living habits to align with the new, evolved soul you want to become.

I started this process of waking up at 26, and I'm now 56. I've been on this journey for 30 years. It takes time. It doesn't happen overnight. I think our society is scared of individual empowerment, so there is a big surge of: "Let's try to control because we are afraid of where this might go."

Some people want to go back to the 1950s, when the government and society could control and limit, before the internet opened up many of the dark corners of society. It is an understandable fear response to the unknown.

Fear is so effective because it unites people to revert to base survival patterns and instincts. Our brains are hardwired for negativity, making fear a powerful motivator. People are more likely to take action when fear is sensationalized. If we can get somebody to feel a fear response, we can get them to be compliant. It's automatic. They are going to fight-flight-freeze-fawn responses.

But the more you do this work, the more you can stand up to the bully within you and around you. You can observe fear when you are more conscious, and you can pause and be intentional in your choice of action. You can shift that energy and let love lead instead of fear.

This is why Dr. Martin Luther King Jr. was so powerful. He led with love. We could make an argument that this is why Jesus was so powerful. He led with love and mercy. We have forgotten that.

(Those last few sentences were channeled. It didn't come from me, it came from somewhere else.)

From Their Bones I Rise

The last six months have been absolutely horrendous. There's no sugarcoating it; it's been rough. But somewhere in the middle of writing this book, it hit me: I wouldn't have been able to share any of this if it weren't for my two sons, Zachery and Noah.

Being their mom has taught me more than I could've imagined. And Paul, my husband of 35 years, has been by my side through it all, steady and supportive every step of the way.

This chapter of my life isn't new, though. The real work began 20 years ago, back in 2005, when I was 36 and finally decided it was time to start healing. I thought I had done the heavy lifting, but healing isn't a straight line.

When 2025 came around, I learned my dad was seriously ill, and all the emotional groundwork I thought was settled began to shift. The news brought up waves of emotion I wasn't expecting. Even after all these years, I found myself falling back into old patterns. Stress, especially the kind that comes with the potential loss of a parent, has a way of dragging things up from deep inside.

When I went to visit him to help prepare his will, I thought I was simply showing up to offer support. But, instead, I ended up meeting younger versions of myself. There was the 3-year-old, whom I've come to call "Care Free." She had once been light and playful, but somewhere along the way, she had lost her spirit. Then the 5-year-old showed up too, the one who had learned to protect herself from adults who were supposed to keep her safe. These parts of me had been tucked away for years, waiting quietly for their chance to be seen.

In the midst of this, I had an image appear: an emu egg sitting at the center of my heart. If you've ever seen one, you know how thick and tough their shells are. You have to really hit them to crack them open. Mine wasn't fully broken, but it had the tiniest fracture. And that, I realized, was enough to start.

Then came Costa Rica, back in January. I had no idea how much that trip would stir up, how deeply it would shake something loose. During a session with Tito, working with his *Khipu*, he tapped my chest with a carved condor-beak rattle, repeating: "Open, open, open." It hurt and left a bruise on me, but something deeper shifted. I didn't know it then, but that was the moment everything quietly began to unravel. It was also the moment it all began again.

At some point in the session, Tito asked me a question that still echoes in me: "Why is your soul here?" I mean, I know the general answer, we're here to learn, to grow, to live through contrast. But lately, it has felt like a lot. The weight of the world is becoming increasingly difficult to bear.

When Kim passed away from breast cancer, something strange and beautiful happened; she showed up. In spirit. Clear, unmistakable. And she had a message: "You're meant to be a death doula." At first, I didn't know what to do with that. I'd had death doulas as clients before, people who could feel spirits, sense the presence of those who had crossed over. But now, these kinds of experiences were happening in my own practice, more often and vividly than ever before.

It started subtly. In brainspotting sessions and intensives, loved ones who had passed away would often appear. At first, it caught me off guard, but then clients started talking, processing, and healing with them. People began reaching out not just for trauma work, but saying things like, "I want to get in touch with my great-grandfather." These weren't just memories surfacing; they were living conversations across time. And with them came a clear theme: the need to heal the lineage line.

That's when I began to question why this was only becoming clear now. Why has this thread been so present and yet so overlooked?

At the same time, I found myself drawn to the work of Daniel Foor. His book *Ancestral Medicine* found its way back into my hands, and I enrolled in one of his classes (Foor, 2017). I was also working closely with Tito, helping navigate this deepening path.

Both speak about creating sacred relationships with our ancestors, not just to honor them, but to engage them in the work of healing. This isn't abstract or fluffy. It's embodied and sacred. Foor writes, "Healthy ancestral engagement helps restore the heart, the soul, the deep mind, and the blood."

That lands deeply for me. This kind of work is an act of liberation, both for us and for them.

Later, while driving to Milwaukee for training, I listened to *Listening When Parts Speak* by Tamala Floyd (Floyd, 2024). I already knew the book; I had used it in my brainspotting and mastermind groups, but hearing it again on that drive hit differently. Floyd also talks about ancestral medicine, and suddenly, I could feel it all coming together. The spiritual messages, the client sessions, and the ancestral work. It wasn't random; it was a path forming under my feet.

I sat down for my own brainspotting session and something inside me cracked open. One of my spirits came through and directly told me, "You have to go through this. All of it. You can't guide others through the layers unless you've walked through them yourself."

A few hours later, I felt a strong urge to look up Daniel Foor again. And of course, he had a new class starting soon. It felt like a confirmation; all the pieces began to fit together. After months of questioning whether I still wanted to do this work, I felt rooted and seen again. As if I had finally found my place, I feel like I'm home.

With that clarity came the understanding of why I've been afraid to share parts of my story. As a kid, I used to see things: white outlines, flowing light, and not faces, but forms. I could also hear them, even if I didn't know what clairaudience meant back then. I'd try to tell my parents, and they would brush it off or shut it down. That dismissal taught me to doubt what I knew to be real. And yet, here I am, full circle, the things I was afraid to say out loud are now central to the work I do with others.

I know not everyone will get it. Some will come to me skeptical. But that's okay, I don't need to convince anyone. I've seen what I've seen. I've felt it.

Tito has been guiding me gently through this process and helping me understand the many paths that are opening. He speaks of the dead with tenderness and honesty, acknowledging why people are hesitant to work with them. "Most of them are unwell," he told me. And he's right; this is why boundaries and discernment matter, but it's also why this work is so important.

Sometimes it's not the most immediate ancestors who step forward to guide us. It might be someone farther back in the line, someone who has done their healing and can now help us do ours. What I've come to see is that the ancestors want to help and are invested in our healing. There is energy passed down through blood and memory, and so many of us are carrying pain that didn't begin with us, but that we can drive to its end.

I've been feeling a strong pull to reconnect with my great-grandfather. Not just out of curiosity, but because I feel that he holds a key to something I need to heal. And I'm not alone in feeling a pull from a long-dead relative. More and more clients are coming in with that same knowledge, that urge to trace their pain and healing back through time, to places the body remembers even when the mind doesn't.

Both sides of my family carry a lot of trauma. Heavy, unspoken, inherited.

And growing up, whenever I tried to name it, I was met with the same dismissive refrain: "Every family has trauma."

Maybe you've heard that one too: a phrase that shuts doors and turns vulnerability into weakness. But someone in every family has to say, "This ends with me."

And in mine, that someone has been me.

I have always been the one to speak the truth. I'm the only one who names it plainly, reminding my family that there's trauma here, and it's unresolved. I've come to believe my parents carry PTSD, though it's never been diagnosed or really talked about. I see how fear runs their lives, how it keeps them small, stuck, and disconnected. They don't feel free, and they don't know why. But I do. I see and feel it.. I am not judging here. I wish all of my family could experience true freedom. I have chosen to do something different.

Because now I understand that I was never broken. I was being prepared.

A few months ago, we visited my parents. It was one of those practical trips, getting paperwork together, helping them organize their will, all the life admin that no one really wants to think about, but we all have to face eventually.

Over the weekend, I noticed that my dad, without even realizing it, kept bringing up the subject of money. Not just once or twice, but constantly: the cost of this, how expensive that was, what something used to cost.

At first, I brushed it off, but by the end of the weekend, it was clear that a thread was running through every conversation. It was about scarcity and fear. And it's not his fault, it's in the lineage. My grandparents were extremely poor. My mom's side struggled a lot, and while my dad grew up with a little more stability, being from a nearly middle-class background, there were always complicated dynamics around money. I see it now in my own life, and even in my kids. That fear, that "not enough" story, it's sticky, it travels.

If I'm being honest, I never really learned how to handle money either. Budgeting and planning weren't modeled for me. I didn't prioritize learning them, so even now, as I try to believe in abundance, I still feel the echoes of that anxiety. I'm working on it. But it's so deep I can feel it in my cells.

So, it's no wonder there's an energy around money that feels tight and tense. I remember growing up and hearing, "We can't afford that," over and over again.

Even today, I catch myself flinching at big purchases or feeling stressed, although it doesn't make logical sense. I see it in a lot of my clients as well, especially the healers. Money is a massive block. There's so much shame and scarcity tied to something that, at its core, is just energy. Just looking at the world we live in, we can notice that hierarchies are everywhere. But why are there levels? Why do some get treated with dignity and others don't? Why can't we move toward unity consciousness?

That's the kind of shift I want to be part of. That's the energy I want to help move. And now I know that it's part of my work.

Working with Tito has recently opened many doors. He has been helping me explore different consciousness paths, asking not just what I want to do, but what resonates with my energy. He talks about roles: Healer, dimension traveler, and other paths I've never even considered. I'm learning that some people are meant to walk between dimensions. Some people are here to help bridge worlds. And I think I might be one of them.

Still, the old stories creep in. I'm 56, as of writing this, and just now putting language to some of this. There's that whisper: "Am I too old for this?" But I know that's not real. It's a false story. I have never been more ready.

I think back to this past January, when Tito asked me: "Why is your soul here?"

We were discussing the world, how it feels lost, and how disconnected people are. And I remembered this moment from my childhood. I must have been seven or eight years old. I was holding this little globe in my hands, crying, asking God and the Earth why people do what they do.

Even then, I could feel something wasn't right, because I've always been connected to something deeper and unseen.

I now understand that wounded people wound others. Yo've heard it said, hurt people hurt people. That we are here to experience contrast and duality, to learn. But still, it's getting harder to watch what's happening in the world and not feel the pain of it, the separation, and forgetfulness. So Tito and I decided to do something about it.

We're creating a documentary. Currently titled *Kutimuy,* a Quechua word tied to the Solar Path, calling you back to your true essence of who you really are.

I see us submitting it to National Geographic. A cultural expedition into the living heart of Andean wisdom, centered on the seven ancestral Inca prophecies. Tito is the 17th Inca of the Solar Lineage, and this project will share that sacred knowledge with the world.

More than a film to Tito, it's a call to humanity. A reawakening through ceremony, Indigenous wisdom, and the stories of those who are remembering who they are. Co-led by the people who carry this tradition, including elders, master healers, and a beautiful, diverse circle of seekers from around the world.

The people involved in the proposal are part of the unfolding. My videographer, Josh, and his business partner, Dan, are on board. They own Shaman Motion Pictures and will be filming and editing the documentary. Teri Nehring, a licensed counselor who now lives in Costa Rica and has been bringing people to Peru for years, has joined the team.

And then there's Tito, Tupac, and Wilka Picchu, the three brothers who guide so many of the travelers who arrive in Peru not knowing why they came, only to realize their souls were leading them there all along.

And now, here we are. Sharing it with others.

As I write this, I have just spent four hours on the grant application, and I'm exhausted. But I know this is what I'm meant to do. The deadline is Monday, and this is happening.

This is the Solar Path. This is the invitation. This is the work.

I recall feeling a deep longing to help people wake up when I was a child. Throughout my entire life and career, my desire has shaped me. I've always known there is more to this world than we see, and I have aimed to help people remember that too.

Recently, in my morning consulting training group, I shared what's next for me: brainspotting and working with the dead. When I mentioned it, the entire group went silent.

Still, they could feel something shift, and then the Spirit channeled through me to come out and share more of this in the book. I'm actually being nudged right now to put on my bilateral music.

(Hang on. Done. Just heard "Breathe" from Cindy Smith's Bodi Tree Bilateral playlist.)

If I'm teaching you about authenticity, about walking through fear, how could I not walk through mine too?

Writing this book has brought up every one of the same old stories: Will they like me? Will I belong? Will I be judged? And I know I'm not the only one carrying these questions. You might be holding them too. That's why I'm sharing all of this with you and why it matters.

Some of you will feel a deep "yes" reading these words. Some might think it's weird. And both reactions are okay.

Brainspotting seemed weird to me at first, too. That's what we do with the unknown; if it doesn't fit in the box of what we deem normal, we label it as strange or dismiss it altogether. But just because we can't see something doesn't mean it's not real.

In Daniel Foor's group, I remember him saying, "This knowledge has been lost. No one taught me this. If I'd had this growing up, imagine where I'd be."

That hit me hard because lately, I've been thinking a lot about my dad. I've wondered if part of the reason I'm being led down this path of working with ancestors and supporting others through death is to help me prepare for his eventual transition. To be grounded, loving, and clear when the time comes.

I recently had to come to peace with the fact that he's not ready to move up to Wisconsin, although I'd hoped he'd spend his final years surrounded by family. My main goal in bringing my parents closer was to give them that. I wanted to share holidays, make memories, and even create a relationship with great-grandchildren. We do not know what tomorrow brings.

We don't know how long he has left. It could be years or months. But I know now that this path I'm walking has meaning. The lessons are here so I can support others through their own grief, ancestral healing, and goodbyes. Not just the death of a loved one, but the death of old identities, untruths, and all that no longer serves.

All of this is vulnerable to say, but I believe the things we're afraid to speak about are often the very things our clients, friends, and families are hiding too. So I'm going first. So you know you're not alone.

Maybe you're starting to feel something flutter inside as you're reading. That's your intuition, a spark, a knowing. Perhaps you're not fully awake yet, but you sense a stirring, and you must follow it.

This book, these words, they carry energy. If you're drawn to them, that means something. There's a calling here, and it might stretch you like it stretched and is still stretching me. Spirit channeled this paragraph through me. These are not my words.

In a recent brainspotting session, I started working with my five-year-old self again. The emu egg came up, and something happened: it felt as if I was going inward while Spirit was coming through. And then I heard it clearly: "Share this."

This was new for me, as for a long time, I'd received these messages and told myself, "It's just me making it up."

But now it feels different. It's not just a message, but direction and guidance. And I'm starting to trust it.

I know other authors out there have channeled wisdom, such as Abraham Hicks' work (Hicks, 2025), or Neale Donald Walsch's *Conversations with God: An Uncommon Dialogue* (Walsch,1996). I just never thought I'd be one of them. But maybe this is what it looks like when we stop doubting and start listening.

> Dear Healers,
>
> Please don't forget yourselves. As you hold space for your clients, community, and ancestors, remember that you, too, deserve a safe house for your soul. A place where your spirit can continue to grow and unfold.
>
> You are a vessel for healing, not meant to absorb it all or be a dumping ground for another's pain. Holding the space supports the possibility for their spirit's healing.
>
> You're not alone in this. When you're holding that sacred container, you're not just doing it solo; there are grandmothers, grandfathers, guides, and guardians present. This isn't just poetic language, it's real.
>
> Love,
> Spirit

The more I have stepped into this work, the more I know it in my bones. And when your clients finally feel safe enough to surrender, their subcortical wisdom will start to rise. That can look wild, and even feel like chaos, but don't be scared, because they probably will be. That's when they need you the most to stay grounded and present, and keep walking with them.

Let me give you an example from my own path…

Within the past year, I was at a training, performing a demonstration with a volunteer. A mother who had lost a child. As soon as we began, I heard a whisper: "Please help my mommy."

And in my head, I responded: "Yes, I'll do my best. Be with us."

I didn't say it out loud, of course, but I could feel the presence of the child, the urgency, and love. They wanted their mom to be able to grieve, to open her heart again. Children don't just disappear; they grow up on the other side.

Sometimes I'll hear a message or a phrase I never would have thought of on my own, and although I don't see them with my eyes, I hear them. That's called clairaudience. Sometimes I get images, but mostly words and feelings. And even though other practitioners can see spirits clearly, I only saw outlines as a child, bright white silhouettes that I couldn't make sense of, but I could always feel.

Another time, during a brainspotting intensive, a client told me they suddenly felt warmth on their back in the middle of a session. At that moment, I heard, "Their grandfather is hugging them," and seconds later, they said aloud, "I see my grandfather."

These moments aren't just memories. They're bridges. Ancestors appear when someone is finally ready to release the presences that are carriers. The ones born to help transmute what couldn't be processed before.

And carriers don't just feel the pain, they carry the gifts too. We're just so conditioned to focus on what's broken that we often overlook what's blooming.

I know both sides of the coin intimately. There's been horrible trauma on both sides of my family, and still, I feel this massive luminous love coming through me as I write this; a deep ache for humanity to remember how precious we are.

That's what I want you to know, and what this book and the upcoming documentary are really about.

A call to remember.

Because we are so often on autopilot that we forget, but when we pause long enough to look, we can finally see it all clearly.

Not everyone will understand this path. Some will scoff or label it something negative or cynical. However, remember that what we label as strange is often simply what doesn't fit into our current worldview. And maybe that worldview is too small. We need to expand our minds to what is possible.

A while ago, I had to come to terms with something heartbreaking: sometimes we can't bring people closer to us in the ways we hope. Yet I've been shown, intuitively, that part of my calling is to help others in their transitions, to be present with love when endings come. This work isn't only about the death of the body, but about guiding people through all kinds of death, of identities, roles, relationships, and even supporting connections with those who have already passed..

These things I'm saying are deeply vulnerable, but I know that if I'm being asked to teach authenticity and fearlessness, I've got to live it too. This work we do isn't just about trauma, it's about lineage. And my own is messy, haunted, and very much real. There's history in my family; my great-grandmother, grandmother, and mother all knew certain things were happening in the family, and no one stopped them, leaving a kind of wound that resides in the bones. And that is what I'm here to clear, not just for me, but for them too.

The grief, rage, and silence they all live in me. But so do the songs, resilience, and wild wisdom that somehow never died.

I have spent years doing this work, and it still isn't gone or at complete peace. That's how I know it's deeper than me. It's in my DNA, in my genetics, and my bloodline. And yet, I'm not trapped by it. I can feel their presence, but I also have a choice. For years, I wanted to run from my lineage; I wanted to be clean and untouched. But now, I'm learning to turn toward it and ask: "What do you need me to understand?"

I can see them sometimes hovering like outlines. The walking dead. Shame. Guilt. Collapse.

But I believe we can interrupt that pattern, so that the living can live feeling clearer, lighter, and more like themselves. And that's what happens when I sit with others and we brainspot their ancestors, something shifts.

Recently, I had a profound session where I learned something unexpected: how to set boundaries with the dead who are still carrying unrest in my lineage.

At first, the work was challenging; it took me several sessions before I was finally able to connect with an ancestor I had never known in my lifetime. Yet when she appeared, I could sense immediately that she had walked a path of healing.

She felt ancient, carrying the wisdom of centuries, and I sensed her roots reaching back to Scotland or Ireland. A woman deeply attuned to the natural world, one who could speak with animals, she knew the language of the land and its healing properties. She did not come alone. Others accompanied her, ancestors who had also carried the torch of healing through the generations.

What struck me most was the contrast. The more recently departed carry so much of our family's unhealed pain. It's as if, somewhere in the not-so-distant past, something important was lost, a thread unraveled, and I'm still learning how to pick it up again. I'm new to working intentionally with my ancestral dead, still tuning my ear to what my ancestors and these energies are trying to teach me.

Reading *The Others Within Us* by Robert Falconer (Falconer, 2023), I was relieved to discover I'm not alone; other practitioners are witnessing these same patterns, these same mysterious overlaps between ancestral wounds and what shows up in our clients and ourselves.

But what really fills me with hope is realizing that this isn't mine to carry alone. Other healers are walking this path, and there are also ancestors, those ancient ones, who are already working in the spirit realms. Their wisdom, resilience, and love are at work, guiding the healing of those who have passed more recently.

This understanding feels like grace. To know I'm supported, that the strength and songs of my lineage move through me, is deeply comforting. When I meditate or use brainspotting, I can sense them, sometimes as whispers, sometimes as feelings, right in my bones. I see flashes of images as sensations move through my body. I don't just hear their stories; I feel their presence as a living force within me.

This work reminds me that healing is not a solitary act but rather a sacred collaboration across time, weaving past and present, spirit and flesh. And with every step I take, I walk alongside those who came before, carrying their wisdom forward into a future where the wounds of the past no longer have the final word.

What amazes me most in these moments is the sense of partnership across time. Healing doesn't have to be a lonely, heroic journey of one; it is an invitation into a relationship. With the living, yes, but just as much with the unseen hands and kind hearts working behind the veil. Sometimes, all it takes is a request. A soft word in meditation, a breath in the middle of brainspotting, or simply an honest admission that I need help. Then, suddenly, the wisdom of a hundred lifetimes is humming quietly in my bones.

This changes everything. It softens the pressure and replaces exhaustion with awe. I don't have to "fix" everything; I am a bridge, a listener, a participant in a far greater story. The work is lighter and deeper at the same time.

My ancestors remind me that healing isn't just about resolving pain; it is about reclaiming lost joy, reviving old songs, and restoring the strength that belongs to us all.

Now, when I sit with clients or reflect on my own heart, I know I'm part of a larger medicine circle. None of us is doing this work alone. We are joined, quietly, surprisingly, sometimes with an unmistakable sense of being held by those who loved before us, those who healed before us, and those who still dream our healing into being. And for that, I am profoundly grateful.

Another recent experience involved a client who came online, saying she was terrified of being visible as a business owner. In her session, she suddenly felt herself being hanged as a witch in Salem. Her fear dissolved after processing the ancestral memory with brainspotting, and she was ready to be seen. And the examples I've shared are just a tiny peek into how the work can unfold. It's an adventure we go through every single day.

So know this: you are more powerful than you have ever been told, and you do have access to your own guides, ancestors, and knowledge. Cynicism might come up, but fight to stay open and let curiosity be a doorway to new possibilities.

Five years ago, I never could have imagined writing a book like this. But this path, this voice, this knowing are all mine now.

Client after client. Journey after journey. Peru. The brothers who teach me. The spirits who whisper. This is my story. And I am learning to trust and own it.

Works Cited

About Allan Schore. Right Brain Psychotherapy Institute. (2021, February 8). https://rightbrainpsychotherapy.com/about-allan-schore/

Bartlett, S., & Swart, Dr. T. (2025, August 14). *Neuroscience expert dr. Tara Swart on evidence we can communicate after death and her experience speaking to the dead!.* Apple Podcasts. https://podcasts.apple.com/us/podcast/ neuroscience-expert-dr-tara-swart-on-evidence-we-can/ id1291423644?i=1000721903278

Brown, B. (2010). The Gifts of Imperfection: Let Go of Who You Think You're Supposed to Be and Embrace Who You Are. Hazelden.

Conscious Content LLC2. (2019). *Light in the Darkness.* United States.

Csikszentmihalyi, M. (2008). Flow: The Psychology of Optimal Experience. Harper Perennial Modern Classics.

Damasio, A.(2010). Self Comes to Mind: Constructing the Conscious Brain. Pantheon.

David Grand, Phd. Brainspotting. (2024, October 22). https://brainspotting.com/about-brainspotting/david-grand-phd/

Doty, J. (2024) Mind Magic: The Neuroscience of Manifestation and How It Changes Everything. Avery.

Dr. Lisa Miller. (2021). https://www.lisamillerphd.com/

Dr. Lisa Miller. (2022). The Awakened Brain: The Psychology of Spirituality. Penguin Books Ltd.

Einstein, A. (1950). Out of my later years: Essays. Thames & Hudson.

Falconer, R. (2023). The Others Within Us: Internal Family Systems, Porous Mind, and Spirit Possession. Great Mystery Press.

Foor, D. (2017). *Ancestral medicine: Rituals for personal and family healing.* Bear & Company.

Glossary of terms: The vicarious trauma toolkit: Glossary of terms. Office for Victims of Crime. (n.d.). https://ovc.ojp.gov/program/vtt/glossary-terms

Hanson, R., Mendius, R., Siegel, D. J., & Kornfield, J. (2009). *Buddha's brain: The practical neuroscience of happiness, love & wisdom.* New Harbinger Publications, Inc.

Home. Home of Abraham-Hicks Law of Attraction. (2025, September 19). https://www.abraham-hicks.com/

Hübi, T. (2023). Attuned: Practicing Interdependence to Heal Our Trauma - and Our World. Sounds True.

Keltner, D. (2023). Awe: The New Science of Everyday Wonder and How It Can Transform Your Life. Penguin Press.

Kolk, B. (2014). The Body Keeps the Score: Brain, Mind, and Body in the Healing of Trauma. Viking.

Kotler, S. (2008). Mapping Cloud Nine: Neuroscience, Flow, and the Upper Possibility Space of Human Experience. Sounds True.

Lindberg, C. (n.d.). Mindful co-regulation in relationships: Brainspotting Specialty Workshop. MINDFUL CO-REGULATION IN RELATIONSHIPS: Brainspotting Specialty Workshop - Cherie Lindberg, PHD. https://cherielindberg.com/trainings/brainspotting-training-mindful-coregulation-in-relationships-1-2-2

Maslow, A.H. (1943) A Theory of Human Motivation. Psychological Review, 50, 370-396. http://dx.doi.org/10.1037/h0054346

Minges KE, Redeker NS. (2016) Delayed school start times and adolescent sleep: A systematic review of the experimental evidence. Sleep Med Rev.

Mousavi, Z., Troxel, W.M. (2023) Later School Start Times as a Public Health Intervention to Promote Sleep Health in Adolescents. Curr Sleep Medicine Rep 9, 152–160. https://doi.org/10.1007/s40675-023-00263-8

National Center for Biotechnology Information. (2022, June 2). In brief: Cognitive behavioral therapy (CBT). U.S. National Library of Medicine. https://www.ncbi.nlm.nih.gov/books/NBK279297/

Office For Victims of Crime. (n.d.). What is vicarious trauma?: The Vicarious Trauma Toolkit: OVC. Office for Victims of Crime. https://ovc.ojp.gov/program/vtt/what-is-vicarious-trauma

Porges, S. W. (2011). *The polyvagal theory: Neurophysiological foundations of emotions, attachment, communication, and self-regulation*. W.W. Norton.

Dr. Sabina Brennan. (2024). The Neuroscience of Manifesting: The Magical Science of Getting the Life You Want. Orion Spring.

Schore, Dr. A. N. (n.d.). *Affect Regulation and the Origin of the Self.* Dr. Allan N. Schore. https://www.allanschore.com/books/affect-regulation-and-the-origin-of-the-self/

Schucman, H. (2019). A course in miracles: Workbook for students: Manual for Teachers. Course in Miracles Society.

Siegel, D. (1999). The Developing Mind: How Relationships and the Brain Interact to Shape Who We Are. The Guilford Press.

Dr. Shamini Jain. (2025). https://www.shaminijain.com/learn/consciousness-and-healing-initiative

Steele, A. "I'm Glad You're Here". Imaginal Nurturing for Women.

Swart, T. (2019) The Source: The Secrets of the Universe, the Science of the Brain. Vermilion.

Ten guideposts for wholehearted living. Brené Brown. (2023, November 14). https://brenebrown.com/art/ten-guideposts-for-wholehearted-living-2/

T'ito, I. (2018). The Main Path of Initiation of the Cosmic Being, into the Secrets and Universal Mysteries of the Pacha. ESI - Inkan Solar School.

Venice Family Clinic. (n.d.). Emotional effects of Secondary & vicarious trauma of medical clinicians. VFC Street Medicine. https://venicefamilyclinic.org/street-medicine/taking-social-medicine-to-the-unsheltered/provider-self-care-and-related-topics/emotional-effects-of-secondary-and-vicarious-trauma-of-medical-providers/

Wahlstrom, Kyla. (2016) Why Teen Brains Need a Later School Start Time. The Conversation.

Walker, Tim. (2022) Later School Start Times More Popular, but What Are the Drawbacks? NEA, 1

Dec. www.nea.org/nea-today/all-news-articles/
later-school-start-times-more-popular-what-are-drawbacks

Walsch, N. D. (1996). Conversations with God: An uncommon dialogue
(Book 1). G. P. Putnam's Sons.

Wheaton AG, Chapman DP, Croft JB. (2016) School Start Times,
Sleep, Behavioral, Health, and Academic Outcomes: A Review of the
Literature. J Sch Health.

Wisner, Wendy. (2023) The Role of Sleep in Teen Mental Health.
Verywell Mind, Verywell Mind. www.verywellmind.com/
teen-sleep-habits-deprivation-causes-effects-7094173

"What Is Polyvagal Theory?" (Accessed 2025, August
1) Polyvagal Institute. www.polyvagalinstitute.org/
whatispolyvagaltheory#:~:text=Polyvagal%20Theory%20
emphasizes%20the%20role,to%20a%20healthy%20human%20
experience

About the Author

Cherie Lindberg, PhD, LPC, is a transformational coach, speaker, advisor, and psychotherapist with over 20 years of experience guiding individuals to their highest expression of who they are, personally, professionally, and spiritually. She holds a PhD in Behavioral Health, is a Licensed Professional Counselor (LPC), and has earned her Master's in Counseling Education, providing her a strong foundation in both clinical expertise and whole-person healing.

Cherie is the founder of *Elevated Life Academy*, a heart-led educational platform for healers, leaders, and changemakers, and the owner of Cherie Lindberg, LLC, a coaching and consulting business devoted to conscious transformation, trauma-informed leadership, and embodied growth.

As a brainspotting trainer and consultant, Cherie weaves brainspotting and parts work with a spectrum of leading-edge modalities. Her approach is deeply integrative—blending neuroscience with consciousness, mindset coaching with performance enhancement, and daily practices with spiritual alignment. She works at the level of both the nervous system and the soul, helping clients rise into wholeness.

At the heart of Cherie's work is a sacred mission: ***to awaken high-performing healers, leaders, and changemakers who are ready to break free from outdated patterns, reclaim their energy, and step fully into embodied leadership.*** Her work is grounded, compassionate, and laser-focused on helping others align their inner healing with their outer impact.

Rooted in the ancestral wisdom of Peruvian and Celtic traditions, Cherie's practice honors the sacred within, guiding clients to reconnect with their intuitive intelligence, clearing the imprints of developmental, collective, and ancestral trauma, and aligning with their deepest inner knowing. This is the space where manifestation becomes magnetic and transformation becomes inevitable.

Cherie's journey is also profoundly personal. Having lived through PTSD, childhood trauma, and the grip of limiting beliefs, she discovered brainspotting as a profound tool for her own healing. That lived experience fuels her work—and her unwavering belief that healing is possible for everyone.

Beyond her professional roles, Cherie has been married for 35 years and is a proud mother of two sons. A passionate animal lover, she finds joy in spiritual practice, learning from diverse cultures, and forming meaningful connections in her community.

Through Cherie Lindberg, LLC, private coaching intensives, 1-2-1 and group coaching, relationship coaching, consulting for conscious organizations, and speaking on global stages, Cherie is here to activate your potential, help you trust your truth, and support you in leading with clarity, courage, and compassion.

Whether you're a seasoned healer or just beginning your journey, Cherie's message is clear: You can heal. You can rise. And you are not alone.

www.ingramcontent.com/pod-product-compliance
Lightning Source LLC
Chambersburg PA
CBHW061754120626
46550CB00005B/1990